PEC

M000036369

Steve Carter

BROADWAY PLAY PUBLISHING INC
224 E 62nd St, NY, NY 10065
www.broadwayplaypub.com
info@broadwayplaypub.com

PECONG

© Copyright 1993 by Steve Carter

All rights reserved. This work is fully protected under the copyright laws of the United States of America. No part of this publication may be photocopied, reproduced, stored in a retrieval system, or transmitted, in any form or by any means, electronic, mechanical, recording, or otherwise, without the prior permission of the publisher. Additional copies of this play are available from the publisher.

Written permission is required for live performance of any sort. This includes readings, cuttings, scenes, and excerpts. For amateur and stock performances, please contact Broadway Play Publishing Inc. For all other rights please contact the author c/o B P P I.

Cover photo by Roger Lewin/Jennifer Girard Studio

I S B N: 978-0-88145-107-8

First printing: May 1993
This printing: September 2016

Book design: Marie Donovan
Page make-up: Adobe Indesign
Typeface: Palatino

The world premiere of PECONG was produced by Chicago's Victory Gardens Theater (Dennis Zacek, Artistic Director) at the Ruth Page Dance Center on 9 January 1990 with the following cast and creative contributors:

GRANNY ROOT...Pat Bowie
MEDIYAH..Celeste Williams
CEDRIC... Gary Yates
PERSIS...Catherine Slade
FAUSTINA .... Wamdachristine
CREON PANDIT ....Ernest Perry Jr
SWEET BELLA...Diane White
JASON ALLCOCK ....Daniel Oreskes
OPPIDANS ....Feleccia C Boyd, Shanesia L Davis, Lydia R Gartin, Shawn Goodwin, Thomas W Greene, V, Alison Halstead, Dexter L Warr, Christopher Williams

Director ....Dennis Zacek
Set designer .... James Dardenne, U S A A
Costume designer ....Claudia Boddy, U S A A
Lighting designer .... Robert Shook, U S A A
Sound designer/stage manager .... Galen G Ramsey
Composer/percussionist ....Willy Steele
Choreographer ....T C Carson
Assistant Director.............................. Sandra Jean Verthein

DIRECTOR'S NOTE
(Chicago—1992)

In Steve Carter's PECONG, we are introduced to
two worlds"Trankey Island and Miedo Wood Island.
Trankey Island is also referred to as "Ile Tranquille"
and as such it is contrasted with the dark sphere of
Miedo Wood. At the end of ACT ONE, darkness has
started to descend on the characters of JASON and
MEDIYAH, conjuring many images including those of
the first man and the first woman on the planet Earth.

PECONG contains abundant references to sleep and
dreams and has the potential to affect an audience on
both a conscious and sub-conscious level. Mr Carter
clearly refers to the environment as an "island of the
mind" in the Caribbean. As PECONG begins, we
encounter MEDIYAH asleep on a pallet and as the play
ends, GRANNY ROOT and MEDIYAH move to Miedo
Wood Island, where GRANNY ROOT concludes with
the final words, "Me spirit tire and me can sleep—
now!" she and MEDIYAH have, at long last, found
their place of proper repose. On their journey, they
have presented us with many timeless perceptions
about human behavior, however, they have also had
more than a "lickle fun on the rood to heartbreak and
vengeance".

PECONG is peopled with characters who are almost
never at a loss for words. Wit flourishes, as does the

desire to outwit. Those yearning for a play, written by a contemporary dramatist, which is elevated in style should be more than sated by this Caribbean play. The text inspires creativity. While it is clearly not a musical, Mr Carter's language is rich in musicality. As with Shakespeare, the dialogue is designed to coincide with the thoughts and emotions of the characters. Any less may result in a production far more prosaic than the author intended. It is no coincidence that GRANNY ROOT has chosen to curse CREON by causing his daughter, SWEET BELLA, to be born "without voice". To be called "Sweet Bella, The Silent" in a world peopled by such richly articulate characters is a hardship of the greatest severity.

Dennis Zacek
Victory Gardens Theater, 1990

CHARACTERS & SETTING

In order of appearance:

MEDIYAH, *Obeah Queen*

GRANNY ROOT, *her grandmother, also Obeah Queen*

CEDRIC, *twin brother to* MEDIYAH

PERSIS, *an island woman*

FAUSTINA, *sister to* PERSIS *and a minor prophetess*

CREON PANDIT, *the own-all, do-all and existing Grand King Calabash*

SWEET BELLA, THE SILENT, *daughter to* CREON

JASON ALLCOCK, *a visitor from a neighboring island*

DAMBALLAH, *played by the actor portraying* CREON PANDIT

Townspeople, dancers, musicians, etc. The number of townspeople can vary from theater to theater.

It has been done with as few as two and three musicians but it does tend to make the production look rather spare.

Time: Well in the past.

Place: Trankey Island (Ile Tranquille), an "island of the mind" in the Caribbean.

This play is dedicated, with love,
to my family. My mother, Carmen,
my sister, June, my nephew Scott,
my nephew Steven and his wife,
Denise, "de niece", and my two
grandnephews, Steven, II and
Leeland

Many special thanks to my friends
Jerry, Sandy and Alexandra Shinner Wilson
and
Zachary, Dennis and Marcie McVay Zacek
and
all the very special staff at
The Victory Gardens Theater
and to Michelle Swanson, "Ms Wonderful",
thanks for being in the Boyce's pool
at just the right time

Written through the courtesy of the Marianne and
Michael O'Shaughnessy Playwrights' Development
Fund with grateful appreciation

PROLOGUE

(The wee hours before cockcrow on a lushly verdant Caribbean "island of the mind". On the floor of a hut, MEDIYAH sleeps on a pallet. Lantern in hand, GRANNY ROOT, enters, thrice circles the figure of her sleeping granddaughter, utters some "mysterious" words and gestures, symbolically. MEDIYAH stirs.)

MEDIYAH: Is you, Granny?

GRANNY ROOT: Who else?

MEDIYAH: I try to stay up, but you was gone so long, I had was to doze off.

GRANNY ROOT: Plenty to do. Get up from there and wise the sleep from you eye. We have t'ing and t'ing to do and we ain't have much time.

MEDIYAH: I ain't want this t'ing to happen.

GRANNY ROOT: It have to pass, Darlin'. This old heart done beat long pass she time. These old bone, them, tired. Is about time this body get throw in the dirt and cause new tree and food to grow.

MEDIYAH: But, I ain't want you to die.

GRANNY ROOT: Ain't I done told you I ain't like that word? I ain't want you to use it! Ain't I done tell you I goin' alway be with you? Is through you, you old Granny goin' live forever.

MEDIYAH: I know you say this, but how I know it true?

GRANNY ROOT: You callin' Granny, "Liar", to she face?

MEDIYAH: I ain't mean it that way. I just want to know if I reach me hand, I could touch you?

GRANNY ROOT: Better than that! Better than anybody "touch"! You goin' feel Granny. Granny goin' be there!

MEDIYAH: I goin' see you?

GRANNY ROOT: Only you, Darlin'. Only you.

MEDIYAH: You make me promise?

GRANNY ROOT: I goin' told you this one last time. You goin' see Granny when you want to see she. Granny goin' let you see she when she want you to see she. And since Granny always goin' want you to see she, you goin' see she. No make me say that again. Now, give me you ear. Time flyin'. Is a lot of thing I never tell you.

MEDIYAH: I all the time know that when you want me to knew thing, you goin' tell me and if you ain't want me to know thing, you ain't goin' tell me.

GRANNY ROOT: Well, you Granny goin' meet she maker and still she no say too much, but certain thing you have to do. Certain thing you have to know. Is only one person in this world I ever love like you and that is you mother. I try me best to love you brother, but is you take me heart. You is you mother all repeat. Cedric have too much of he father in he.

MEDIYAH: But, Granny, Cedric and me…twin. We have the same daddy.

GRANNY ROOT: You hear what I say? You is all you mother! Cedric…all he father!

MEDIYAH: Yes. Cedric even look like…

GRANNY ROOT: Hush! Don't even utter that name! We ain't never mention that name! If you have suspicion, keep it in you head and you heart. You ain't need that

name in you mouth. Now, we have to go past all that
'cause t'ing already set in motion. I been out doin' and
doin'. Come here to me!

(GRANNY ROOT, *firmly, grasps* MEDIYAH'*s arms.*)

GRANNY ROOT: Before,
all you did know, for sure,
was herb and root and bush to cure
a pauper at death door.
Now, darlin' granddaughter,
you goin' know more
Granny leavin' you
for you own appliance,
all she power and she science.

MEDIYAH: Don't leave me, Granny.

GRANNY ROOT: All is ready.
T'ing in motion.
You can't stop tide or wave
in the ocean.
Once you was baby
then, you wean.
So you was Princess,
now…you Queen!
Stand up tall
and wipe you eye.
You is Queen
and Queen don't cry.

MEDIYAH: What about Cedric?

GRANNY ROOT: Cedric is man! Only woman does
have power and knowledge of science in this family.
Nothing Granny can do for Cedric no more. You do
for him what you can, if you willin'. He you brother
and he not a bad sort, but he too much he father and
that same father cause me and you grief. Now hear me
'cause I think it goin' soon day. The minute I shut me
eye, you reach with you hand and pull out me heart.

Wrap it in Tingus leaf while it still beat. If anybody
want, all you could have you funeral funnery and t'ing,
then throw this ol' carcass in the hole that I done dig
out back. Then, you and only you take me heart and
bury she on Miedo Wood Island.

MEDIYAH: Miedo Wood Island? But, Granny, I can't go
there. Nobody can go there. Since I been live on this
earth, only one person me ever see go there and come
back to tell it…and that is you.

GRANNY ROOT: And now, you goin' be the only one go
there.

MEDIYAH: But that place have all wild animal and
serpent and haunt and t'ing.

GRANNY ROOT: Mediyah! You Queen now. No place
hold badness for you. You born on Miedo Wood
Island like you mother before you and me. You have
nothing to fear! You the Queen of Miedo Wood Island.
It belong to you, now. Nothing touch you! And if you
feel to take somebody there…

MEDIYAH: …Somebody?…

GRANNY ROOT: …nothing touch he, either.

MEDIYAH: Granny, what you talkin'?

GRANNY ROOT: Remember, you power is great.
Make you no misuse it,
Make you no abuse it.
Make you no confuse it.
or, dear heart, you could lose it.
But you could have tickle bit of fun, now and then.
I always have tickle fun doin' t'ing to that Faustina
Cremoney. She of the great, trifling effort. But the
Gods, them, know I ain't mean she no real harm. She
can sometime be lickle botheration, but she not too
bad a sort. Have some toleration with people like she.
How-so-ever, if somebody do you a true and harsh

badness, defend youself with all you power. Bring
down rage and destruction. Don't care who it is and
no mind the cost to you, so long you have honor and
standin' when you see you face in you glass. Now,
I goin'. I hear cock stampin' he foot and clearin' he
throat to sound, "Mornin'!". Come! Let Granny caress
you one next time.

MEDIYAH: I ain't want this time to come!

GRANNY ROOT: What I tell you 'bout that, eh? Granny
goin' all the time be with you.
When it dark. When it light.
When it day. When it night.
When it sun. When it storm.
When it breeze. When it warm.
Well, you goin' stand there and let me go to me grave
without kiss?

MEDIYAH: Oh, Granny. Granny.

*(From off-stage, comes the lilting rhythm of Calypso music.
In the distance, a dancing figure clad like a Chanticleer,
struts and prances.)*

GRANNY ROOT: It time! Remember me! Think of me
and you mother and let we have vengeance. Good-bye,
Darlin'.

MEDIYAH: What?

GRANNY ROOT: 'Bye, girl. Now.

*(Suddenly, there is cockcrow and the dancing figure mimics
a real rooster. Simultaneously, GRANNY ROOT lifts her
arms to Heaven, MEDIYAH screams and plunges her hand
into GRANNY ROOT's chest and pulls out her pulsating
heart. She wraps it in a large leaf as GRANNY ROOT falls
back, lifeless, in her chair. MEDIYAH sinks to the ground at
her grandmother's feet. The scene brightens, just a bit, and
the dancing figure is revealed to be, CEDRIC, twin brother to
MEDIYAH. He is exuberantly tipsy and is accompanied by*

*an entourage that consists of two overly-attentive dancing
ladies and some musicians.)*

CEDRIC: Mediyah! Mediyah! Rouse youself and
make you come out here and greet you brother, The
Champion!
I win again! I win again!
Four time in a row
I win again! I win again!
King of Calypso.
I vanquish all me rival
and scuttle all me foe.
I put then to rout
with sweet word from me mout'.
All I do is sing out
and, down, they go.
Is then when they fin'
this night made for me, one, to shine
And I win again! I win again!
Ain't I told you so?
I win again! I win again!
Four time in a row.
One more time to go
and the permanent title of
Mighty, Royal, Most Perfect, Grand King Calabash
is mine.
Yes, Girl. You shoulda see you brother. I all the time
magnificent and superb, but tonight…I go past that.
Tonight, I sing better than God!
I win again! I win again!
He put them all to shame.
I win again! I win again!
Them too sorry that them came.
Them Saga-boy so wilted
them faint right to the floor
Them kick up them feet
and can't compete

no more!
I win again! I win again!
I lash they with me tongue.
I win again! I win again!
I, King of the Pecong.
I bring home the medal,
the cup and the cash
Higher than high is how I does rate.
Climb out you bed and celebrate.
I win the title four time straight.
One next time and I permanently be the great,
Mighty, Royal, Most Perfect and Grand King Calabash.

(CEDRIC *and his companions are dancing vigorously when,*
MEDIYAH, *now clad in mourning, comes out of the hut with
the wrapped, still beating heart in her hands.* CEDRIC, *on
seeing her, sobers immediately.*)

CEDRIC: All you, less that noise! I say, "Quiet!", nuh?

(*Everyone goes silent, staring at* MEDIYAH.)

CEDRIC: The ol' lady gone, eh?

(MEDIYAH *nods.*)

CEDRIC: She go peaceful?

(MEDIYAH *nods.*)

CEDRIC: She ain't have no pain?

MEDIYAH: No.

CEDRIC: Then, she go good. What more all we could
want? She run a long and good race, so why you look
so baleful. All we have to pass. Who know that better
than she? No, sister…
We ain't have to be sad.
We ain't have to feel bad.
Let we take she and put she in the ground
Pronounce some pleasant word, then prance around.
Let we sing and take libation

then, let we make some tickle celebration.
Mop up you face and let we see you smile.
Granny Root goin' home...in style!
(*He gestures to his musicians.*)
All you boy help me pick she up and tote she to she restin' place.

MEDIYAH: She hole already dig in the yard. Put she in it gentle.

CEDRIC: Where you go?

MEDIYAH: Elsewhere!

CEDRIC: What you do?

(MEDIYAH *holds the leaf-wrapped, audibly-beating heart aloft. Thunder and lightning flashes.* CEDRIC *is suddenly, trance-like.*)

CEDRIC: I understand!

MEDIYAH: All you, be gentle with she remains!

(CEDRIC *and the men pick up the corpse and, joined by the two dancing girls, do symbolic, ritualistic movement, then, they exit.*)

(*As* MEDIYAH *prepares to leave,* GRANNY ROOT, *now clad in black veiling and holding a large, opened, black umbrella, trimmed with the same black, floor-reaching veiling, appears.* MEDIYAH *still holds the heart aloft.*)

MEDIYAH: Remember, Granny. You make me a promise to all the time be here.

GRANNY ROOT: And since when Granny Root fail to keep she premise. Granny goin' all the time be with you, Girl.

MEDIYAH: I, the granddaughter of Granny Root.
Let everybody know it.
I, the granddaughter of Granny Root.
Let everybody know it!

(MEDIYAH, *followed by the ghost of* GRANNY ROOT, *exits.*)

(*Lights!*)

END OF PROLOGUE

ACT ONE

Scene One

(Some weeks later. Cock-crow on the island. In her hut,
PERSIS *sleeps on a straw pallet.* FAUSTINA, *her sister and
garbed as befits an Obeah Queen, enters with authority.)*

FAUSTINA: Persis!

PERSIS: What is it, Faustina? I just lay down me head
from me revels and here you come. what you want?

FAUSTINA: Rise, Woman! Is a brand new day.
You want to sleep you life away?

PERSIS: Be-shite!

FAUSTINA: The sun done rise. The cock done cry
It time for you to ope' you eye.

PERSIS: Woman, stop! I sick to death with this rhyme
business. Every mornin' you wake up, you chantin'
rhyme like you is some high priestess or some such.
Just 'cause, all of a sudden, you learn how to read
tickle piece of card and t'ing.

FAUSTINA: Aha! So, that what do you of late? You
jealous 'cause I get the gift. You been so ever since I get
Granny Root card, them. Well, m'dear
I ain't ask and I ain't make deal.
I ain't beg and I sure ain't steal.

PERSIS: There she go again!

FAUSTINA:
I dream Granny Root come to me just 'fore she die
and she voice let out one baleful sigh.
"I goin' soon.", she say. "'Twon't be long,
but you know how I does like me rum strong.
So, if you put a crock o' you best grog 'side me stone,
I goin' leave you the gift of prophecy for you very
own."

PERSIS: Deliver me!

FAUSTINA:
When it come to brewin', you know I better than good.
All the time boil up cane and t'ing better than you
    could.
You act like is me fault that me brew up the best
and make run stronger than you and the rest.
'Taint me fault when me get home and open me door,
me find Granny Root tarot card sittin' on me floor.

PERSIS: I still think you does find them old, worn-out
card in Granny Root trash. Why she leave them to you?
She make rum better than anybody. She ain't have to
seek from you.

FAUSTINA: She did always confess a secret admiration
for me brew.

PERSIS: You too fool and you think me one, the same.
You does march 'round here makin' utterance sound
like they is pronouncement from on high. If Granny
Root let you have them card, she only funnin' with
you like she all the time use to do or she plannin' some
special trick. She ain't leave you no book or potion or
scientific power.

FAUSTINA: Well, after all, I ain't relate to she.
Blood thicker than water.
And all them kind of recipe,
she leave to she black-face granddaughter

PERSIS: You better hush you mouth 'fore Mediyah hear
you and work goozzoo an you hindpart.

FAUSTINA: Long as I wearin' all these amulet,
I ain't have the first thing to fear.
'Sides, that black, monkey-face creature
ain't nowhere near.

PERSIS: Hah! The woman have ear like bat. You better
watch you tongue, 'cause you ain't know what she
capable of. Granny Root all the time say when that girl
come into she own, she goin' be even more powerful
than she. You and me, both, does know that still water
does run deep, deep, deep and all that glitter, far from
gold!

FAUSTINA: And, pray tell, what that does mean?

PERSIS: Nothin'! I just feel to say it. You think you is the
only one could make pronouncement?

FAUSTINA: Well,
speak of the devil and here come she brother.
All fill up with heself...and no other.

PERSIS: Hmmm. He and he entourage!

(*Enter* CEDRIC, *quatro in hand, and his rag-tag band of
followers.*)

PERSIS: Mornin', Mr. Cedric.

CEDRIC: Is me you a-talk to?

PERSIS: Who else passin'?

CEDRIC: If is me you want to address,
you must say, "His Mighty and Royalness".

PERSIS: Oh, man, shut you face, Mister Big Shot. The
rule say you have to win Pecong and Calypso five time
consecutive 'fore you can lay claim to bein' Mighty,
Royal or Grand. You ain't win but four. Only ol' Creon
Pandit and he daddy 'fore he win five time. And, come
what you bet, if Creon did have a boy instead of he

daughter, Sweet Bella, the Silent, them Pandit would
still have claim to the title. Maybe you think you is a
Pandit. Come to think of it… Now that I look…you
does have the look of Creon 'bout you, you know.
'Specially 'round you eye, you nose, you mouth, you
ear, you chin. You ain't think so, Faustina?

CEDRIC: I better than all them Pandit.

PERSIS: Is what you think. You voice like a rasp. I ain't
see how come you win four time…much less…one.
I know the judge them have substance and honor, so
you must be use some big magic or some such to get
them pick you, Mister Cedric.

CEDRIC:
"Cedric, the Magnificent", is no more me name.
I, now, the Mighty, Royal, Most Perfect,
Grand King Calabash of substance and fame.

PERSIS: Oh, God. Save me from this rhyme to-do!

CEDRIC: I, one born calypsonian. Who better to rhyme?
Whomsoever come to challenge me, just waste up they
    precious time.

PERSIS: Shite!

CEDRIC: And what do you, Auntie? How come you so
close-mout'?

FAUSTINA: Ain't none you damn "Auntie",
so no call me such
You can't see what I doin',
Mr. Know-so-much?
You can't see that I readin' card?
Just use you eye. That ain't too hard!

PERSIS: Double shite! Now, the two of them rhymin'.

CEDRIC: Them card look, for all the world, like no other
than them that did belong to me old grandmother.

FAUSTINA: Where them come from is my affair,
'long as I get them fair and square.

PERSIS: Stop! I say, "Stop!"
It like one bad dream.
If I hear one more rhyme,
I goin' scream…
Oh, be-Christ! Them have me doin' it!

CEDRIC: Pay she no mind. Is me you readin'?

FAUSTINA: I just readin', but it look like you in the deck,

CEDRIC: What then say 'bout me?

FAUSTINA: You ain't want to hear.

CEDRIC:
You think I does frighten? You think I does scare?
Nothin' does fright me. Nothin' dare!

(PERSIS, *almost silently, screams.*)

CEDRIC: I think you does forget what is the trut'.
That I is the grandson of Granny Root.

FAUSTINA: That ain't mean a t'ing.
All we know is only the female in you line
that does have power to do science and divine.

CEDRIC: You better tell me now,
you wrinkle-up, ol' cow!

PERSIS: Why you mout' so nasty? Tell he the bad news,
Faustina.

FAUSTINA: I too happy to do so.
These card, them, say, "Some new singer comin' 'roun'
and it look like Cedric goin' down!"

CEDRIC: Who? Who risin' to challenge?
Where the man?
Let he show he face, if him can!
Find me the man so skill at rhymin'!
Find me the man who have the timin'

that this Eighty Calabash possess.
Oh, yes.
Find me the man who can beat me.
If him so willin'
tell the villain
to step forth and try to unseat me.
I raise me sweet voice, loud and clear
and issue challenge to all who can hear
I say to all assemble here
and far and near,
"In melodious combat, come and meet me
and see if you is the one
who can lose he life,
he home, he wife,
he fork, he knife,
he stress, he strife.
The time most rife,
me son,
for tryin' to defeat me.
Defeat me? Hah! Never!
I am the Mighty, Royal, Most Perfect,
Grand King Calabash...forever!

(CEDRIC *and his "groupies" play and dance furiously. Then, at a signal from him, march off.*)

PERSIS: See how then young gal hang off he?
Like them 'fraid to let go he arm.
Like them 'fraid him goin' vanish into thin air.
Like him so much Mr. Charm.

FAUSTINA: Eh-eh! You rhyme?

PERSIS: It contagious.
Him think him the end-all and be-all,
but pride does goeth before the fall.

FAUSTINA: Yes, Miss Adage.
I done already read he card.
Him goin' fall and him goin' hit hard.

PERSIS: You see that, eh?

FAUSTINA: Yes, man. It plain like day.
And when him fall and hit the groun',
is someone from he own house goin' bring he down.
Hahoii! But look who crossin' now.

PERSIS: Them two! Hmmm!

(CREON PANDIT, *followed by his daughter*, SWEET BELLA,
THE SILENT. *She walks seductively, giving the "eye" to
every male she sees.*)

PERSIS: Mornin', Creon Pandit! Mornin', Sweet Bella
Pandit!

(SWEET BELLA *smiles, condescendingly.*)

CREON: All you here as usual, eh? So, what the news?
For I know if there any, all you would know it, 'cause
you all the time on sentry duty like two sentinel. So,
who pass durin' the night? Who doin' rudeness with
who? Who deliver baby for who? Who fart?

FAUSTINA: You ol' buzzard. Me goods come in?

CREON: Them tickle piece of cloth you dogs order been
come into me emporia long time. It there waitin' for
you. You have the cash to pay for it?

FAUSTINA: I have credick. You know I alway pay me
bill.

CREON: Credick, shite! The last time were almost two
year 'fore you pay me.

FAUSTINA: Brute! Who tell you to put me business on
the road. Well, I guess you can't help youself. Is all that
Chinee, Syrian and Indian blood mix up in you.

CREON: What you say?

FAUSTINA: As I does so often say, "Too much strain for
you vein!"

CREON: You ol' Zulu. I ain't have the first piece of Chinee in me.

PERSIS: How you know? You daddy keep record of he ramblin'?

FAUSTINA: And who you callin', "Zulu"? Me ancestor come here straight from Egypt!

CREON: Strike me blue and Holy shite!
Cleopatra think she white!
(He surrenders to convulsive laughter.)

PERSIS: I ain't see nothin' a bit funny. Both of us descend straight from the Nile.

CREON: Ooh-hoo! You hear that, Sweet Bella?
Both of they does come from the Nile.
Well, so does crocodile!
Come! Let we go 'fore these two North African lift up they shift and pull two asp from 'mong them old basket of fig and sic they on we,

FAUSTINA: I readin' you card, Creon Pandit. Somethin' dire goin' befall you.

CREON: Hahoii! Somethin' dire already befall. I see you the first thing this mornin'. What more "dire" than that, eh? Come, Sweet Bella.

(SWEET BELLA, silently laughing, obeys her father and they go off, CREON, still convulsed with laughter.)

She ancestor from Egypt! Is a wonder she even know Egypt. Is a wonder she know Egypt a-tall!

FAUSTINA: *(Calling after him)* The card, them, say you goin' have big trouble.

PERSIS: That man still pretty, you know!

FAUSTINA: He too pretty and he still have plenty big stone for a man he age.

PERSIS: But that don't diminish with age, m'dear. Only it ability to rise up and dance 'round. I still like the way him pant fit he. You ever take he?

FAUSTINA: Is for me to know and you to mind you business. You?

PERSIS: I ain't shame to say. Yes!

FAUSTINA: You too lie!

PERSIS: 'Twas too dear and precious a moment in me life to debate with you. Who comin' next, Miss Oracle?

FAUSTINA: Yes. Change subject. Is Mediyah.

PERSIS: I does feel sorry for she sometimes. She look so sad and different since Granny Root pass. Like she ain't know life. Like she dry.

FAUSTINA: Ain't you would be dry, too, if you ain't never have man for moist you? Man don't want she. It run in the family. Creon Pandit ain't never even think 'bout marryin she mother. Even when he find she carrying she and Cedric in she belly for he.

PERSIS: Careful, Woman! Mediyah might could hear you.

FAUSTINA: She still far off.

PERSIS: Remember she know science and t'ing. She still Granny Root granddaughter.

FAUSTINA: All we know Granny Root the Queen of Science and T'ing, but this grand-daughter ain't she. We ain't have the first sign that the woman pass on she power to this one. She have yet to let we see one tickle miracle. All we know Mediyah know herb and bush for healin', but who ain't know that?

PERSIS: But Mediyah all the time know more than anybody. It come natural to she. And she still the only one can go to Miedo Wood Island for special herb and bush and root and t'ing and come back. Ain't no animal, haunt or t'ing does ever bother she. She charm! Sometime she does talk wild and crazy and when I peep me eye in she window, she 'lone and solitary, but I swear, and on more than one occasion, me hear she sayin' "Granny, this…" and "Granny, that…"!

PERSIS: Hup! It she, for true!

(MEDIYAH *comes on pulling a small boat on wheels, in which the ghost of* GRANNY ROOT *sits with a small earthenware crock of ram, from which she occasionally sips. She is unseen* PERSIS, FAUSTINA *or anyone else on stage except* MEDIYAH *who, unnoticed by* PERSIS, *gives* FAUSTINA *a casual, but significant glance…at which* FAUSTINA *freezes.)*

PERSIS: Hello, Mediyah. Where you a-go on this hot day?

MEDIYAH: Ah? The day feel hot to you? It feel cool to me.

PERSIS: Now that I does hear you say it, it do feel cool.

MEDIYAH: Yes. It cool with just a trifle too much heat.

PERSIS: I notice that. It cool, yet it hot!

MEDIYAH: You was all the time quite perceptive.

PERSIS: So, where you travellin' on this cool, hot day?

MEDIYAH: I goin' where I goin', to do what I goin' do. If you friend, the minor prophetess, could move she mouth, she might could tell you, but I had was to still she for a lickle bit 'cause I ain't care for she tone. Faustina, darlin', I only havin' lickle fun with you 'cause, number one…you no worth me energy or me true power and, number two, I in a very good mood. But you must remember, I ain't never smell fart in me life. You want know why? 'Cause no matter how silent they does come out a person hind part, I able to hear them and move out the way. So you must figure, if I able to hear silent fart, not that I fully comparin' you to a silent fart…mind you, but if I able to hear silent fart, you know I can hear when people say vicious thing 'bout me and me family. You get that? Now, Persis, after I move on, make you count to seven and this ol' rag will regain she speech and movement. She so light in substance, all I need is me thought. alone, to send she to oblivion if me want. She could hear me, it true, but I feel you should tell she. That way, we make sure you know it, too.

(MEDIYAH, *pulling the little boat, goes off.* GRANNY ROOT, *motionless throughout the preceding, now turns to look at the two women and laughs uproariously, but silently. As soon as they're out of sight,* PERSIS *bolts to* FAUSTINA.)

PERSIS: Faustina? Oh, God! Faustina?

((MEDIYAH *returns.)*

MEDIYAH: Oh yes. Tell she to get some tanbark and weave it into a true collar for wear 'round she neck if she want some lickle protection from me. So long, darlin' Persis. So long, Creature.

(MEDIYAH *goes again.)*

PERSIS: Oh, God, God, God! You see what you and you mouth get you? One! Ain't I tell you the woman could hear a mosquito makin' pee-pee on welwet? Two! I tell you the woman have extraordinary power! Three! She know science! She have skill! Four! And you goin' bait she just 'cause you could read lickle piece of card and sign! That ain't power! Five! Is a wonder she ain't change you into a she-goat! Is a wonder she ain't make soldier crab chew on you titty and make wart all over you face! Is a wonder she even tell me to count to seven!

(FAUSTINA *doesn't move.)*

PERSIS: I say, "Seven!". Wait! Maybe I miss. Make I recount. One, Two, Three, Four, Five, Six, Seven! I say it right! Seven ain't the right number. Faustina, I can't break the spell. I 'fraid you done for. I 'fraid you speechless forever. Well, at least you ain't die!

(MEDIYAH, *pulling her boat, returns.*)

MEDIYAH: Ain't I tell you I was funnin'? Now, I goin', for true.

PERSIS: But, wait, kind Mediyah. You tell me the number is seven. I count to seven and me poor sister still ain't move.

MEDIYAH: Oh, yes. I lie! I tell you I was funnin' The number is ten. For true! Better say it fast for she look, for all the world, like she goin' pass monumental gas if she don't let out some word soon.

PERSIS: One, Two, Three…

MEDIYAH: No! You must wait 'till I gone and I ain't in no big rush. I just goin' tra-la-la at me own pace. Take me own sweet time, Tra-la-la, tra-la-la, tra-la-la…

(MEDIYAH, *pulling the cart with the veiled and silently chuckling* GRANNY ROOT, *goes off. This time,* PERSIS *follows her a bit to make sure she's gone.*)

PERSIS: One, two, three, four, five, six, seven, eight, nine…and I home she ain't havin' more hilarity with we this time. Believe me, Faustina, I ain't even see the woman when she put on spell.

(FAUSTINA, *almost out of the spell, looks like she's about to explode. She makes muffled noises and tries to stamp her foot.*)

PERSIS: Oh, yes. Ten!

(FAUSTINA *stomps free of her enforced trance and gasps for breath.*)

FAUSTINA: Bark! Strip me some bark, Woman! The succubus try to turn me to stone. Fetch me piece bark! That damn criminal try to choke me! Bark! Bark!

PERSIS: You ain't learn? You still spoutin' insult?

FAUSTINA: *(In a more cautious whisper)* Fetch me the bark, Woman! The witch…I mean…she…that one try everything she know to take 'way me vitals. Bark, Woman! Hurry, nuh? Fetch me a big piece o' bark!

PERSIS: I fetchin'. I fetchin'.

(PERSIS runs off-stage as FAUSTINA continues gasping for breath. PERSIS returns, carrying some strips of bark from a tree.)

PERSIS: Here!

FAUSTINA: Why you a-hand me them for?

PERSIS: Ain't you yell and scream so 'cause you want it. Ain't you cause me to run 'round like damn wild indian and damn near bruck up me foot lookin' for this damn shitey bark?

FAUSTINA: But, ain't you the one so "Miss Artful" with she hand and needle and thread and t'ing. Weave me a collar, nuh?

PERSIS: You hear the ingrate? "Weave me a collar, nuh?". Well you could tell me when the word, "Please", dis-tappear from the English language, eh?

FAUSTINA: No time for no, "Please"! I think I dyin'.

PERSIS: If wish was dream and you should live so long!

FAUSTINA: Weave, Woman. Weave!

PERSIS: Rass!

(Lights)

Scene Two

(Miedo Wood Island. MEDIYAH, *pulling the boat with* GRANNY ROOT, *enters. Rocks and branches of palm trees are arranged to look like two thrones,* GRANNY ROOT *sits on one of them and seems to be listening for something or someone.)*

MEDIYAH: Okay, Granny, we here. Maybe now you could part you lip and tell me why I have to come here today. I ain't need to come here. I already have enough herb and bush and root in the house where I ain't have to forage for another fortnight or two unless is a breakout of some plague or epidemic or somesuch. Why you have such urgency for this place today?

GRANNY ROOT: Hush, Girl.

MEDIYAH: Why you have you ear on a-cock so for?

GRANNY ROOT: Aha! All in readiness. It soon time.

MEDIYAH: Soon time for what?

GRANNY ROOT: Somebody soon come.

MEDIYAH: Granny, darlin', Everybody, them, know Miedo Wood Island have all sort of haunt and wild animal and t'ing. Who so fool to brave all that by comin' here?

GRANNY ROOT: Somebody brave and fool.

MEDIYAH: Well, whoever 'tis, too much fool for me. I ain't want to meet such.

GRANNY ROOT: Somebody comin'. Granny know! Granny always know! You ain't want to own it, but you does know, too.

MEDIYAH: Sometime I does forget you dead, you know.

GRANNY ROOT: Ain't I told you 'bout usin' that word?

MEDIYAH: I does forget that, too, 'cause ever since you...that word you ain't want me to say, you ain't

leave me 'lone long enough to get use to the fact that
you is really…that word you ain't want me to say.
And, what is more, you ain't been…that word you ain't
want me to say, long enough for me to get use to the
fact that you really…that word you ain't want me to
say. You know what I tryin' to say, Granny darlin'?

GRANNY ROOT: You know, sometime you does miss
you pass. We have to be serious, Girl. I leave lickle
something quite untidy on this earth when me bone
get the call from yonder. I thought I could rectify in me
own time, but voice greater than mine say, "All thing
in they own time!". So, it fallin' to you to take care
of everything for Granny. So it be! Aha! Footfall! He
comin'!

MEDIYAH: He? Man comin' to defy this evil wood?

GRANNY ROOT: *(Chanting)*
You Granny Root granddaughter. You be the best.
You do this thing for Granny, then Granny rest.
You give youself over to all them God of Greatness.
Give youself over to all them old God of Greatness
and Blackness.
Give youself over.
Let they take you.
Give youself over.
let they make you
Granny Root granddaughter, for true
Give youself over.
I goin' be here.
Give youself over.
and let he see, here
Granny Root granddaughter is you.
Give youself over.
Give youself over.
Give youself over.

(There is a flash of lightning and a roll of thunder. For an instant, GRANNY ROOT and MEDIYAH seem to be frozen in time. There is another flash of lightning, more thunder and an agonizing scream from man somewhere in the wood. At that scream, GRANNY ROOT disappears.)

MEDIYAH: Granny, you hear that? But, wait. Where you a-go? Granny? Granny?

GRANNY ROOT *(Off.)*

You ain't need to see me. Go see who scream in the wood?

(MEDIYAH obeys. Shortly after, she comes aiding a young man, with much difficulty. His clothes are torn way to the point where, except for a piece of rag…here and there… he'd be naked. He collapses on the ground at the feet of MEDIYAH.)

MEDIYAH: Oh, God! But you is a pretty piece of flesh!

JASON: Thank you, Missy. Is so woman all the time tell me. Thank you, God, for lettin' a woman be the last thing I see 'fore I pass.

MEDIYAH: Pass? But, you is too pretty to die.

JASON: Me know that, but I think I cashin' in me chips all the same.

MEDIYAH: Well you could tell me you name 'fore you make all you good-bye and t'ing.

JASON: In life I was Jason Allcock from Tougou Island. Known the entire length and breadth of Tougou as, "Jason, The Ram", born-Calypsonian, extraordinaire.

MEDIYAH: Pad tell me, Mr. Jason Allcock, you pretty ram-goat, what you doin' here in this wild, lickle piece of spit in the ocean. This wood have haunt. This Island death to human being. You ain't hear that?

JASON: I am one born-calypso… Oh, I say that already. I come here because a ol' dead-face woman come to

me in a dream and tell me to came here. She say in this
wood does grow the Calabash tree. This Calabash tree
does have the best wood in the entire world to make
quatro. She say, too, that here it does have a cat blacker
than thought...which if I could catch it and rip out she
entrail, it gut does make string for the quatro. She say if
I combine the Calabash wood and the cat gut, I would
have Heaven for a voice and a quatro that sound like
golden harp.

MEDIYAH: And why you must have such?

JASON: For the challenge!

MEDIYAH: What is this, "Challenge" and why it so
important, you risk up you life?

JASON: I hear 'bout this pretender to the throne of
Royal, Mighty, Most Perfect, Grand King Calabash.
Them say him win four time and goin' for five, then
him Calabash for life.

MEDIYAH: I hear such.

JASON: I here to put a stop to that, 'cause no man can
match me when it come to Pecong and t'ing. But this
same ol' woman tell me in the dream, quatro from
this wood not only the best, but make me completely
invincible. I hear this self-same, so-call champion
nightingale get he wood and gut string from here.

MEDIYAH: Is so you hear?

JASON: Is so. This same ol' hag tell me I would know
the tree when I see it, but she no tell me this forest
so brutal and vicious. When I come to this place, a
tempestuous storm lash out at me and overturn me
craft. I had was to swim ashore fightin' and dodgin'
all kind of shark, them. Then I pull meself here and all
kind of wild t'ing snap and spit at me and me clothing
tear off and leave me lookin' like bare-ass pickney.

MEDIYAH: Bare-ass pickney lookin' sweet to these eye.

JASON: Thank you, sweet thing. On a regular day,
I would done long time grab you and pitch you to
the floor and do you a rudeness, but I ain't have the
strength today. I dyin'.

MEDIYAH: Is so you think?

JASON: Well, like I say, all them wild critter does rear
and tear at me, but I fight then off with me cutlass. I
swingin' machete at all of them, but they too numerous
and them chase me right to the Calabash tree, Is just
like that ol' thing say. I know that was the tree. It like
I could see golden quatro dangle from every leaf. I
take me cutlass and I 'bout to fell the tree, when…
yarrak! A cat, bigger and blacker than the universe,
jump from the topmost branch and land 'pon top me.
I tell you, we havin' some punch up before I give she a
final punch. She scream like a ol' woman and fall out.
I slit she open and rip out she gut. Is while I 'tendin' to
this with me back turn, I feel…doop! The damn, dread
Calabash tree cobra strike me a fatal blow. Look you!
You see the mark? So, I ain't have long. And worse yet,
I done leave me wood and me gut in the damn jungle.
This the first time you could call me a fool. I believe
in a dream. I guess I must be goin' now, 'cause you
standin' over me and everything already lookin' dark.

MEDIYAH: What you mean by that, Mister?

JASON: I mean the blacker the berry, the sweeter the
juice. Lord, it make me think.. is only three thing I
regret I ain't do 'fore I kick out. One! I ain't leave no
son. I ain't leave son, the first, behind me!

MEDIYAH: Pretty ram like you?

JASON: I have plenty daughter all over Tougou, but that
ain't no 'complishment.

MEDIYAH: No?

JASON: None of them woman, them, ever bring me boy. All man need son to carry on he name. Gal pretty, but they can't sing Calypso in the tent. The rule say, "No woman for sing in the Calypso tent!".

MEDIYAH: If you dyin' like you say, you wastin' time. What the next two regret?

JASON: I ain't goin' be here to challenge this four-year upstart for the champion-ship. Oh, Woman, if I was not 'bout to meet me creator, I would compose a lickle lilt for you. Words like honey I tell you, For I mellifluous like hell.

MEDIYAH: Ah hah!

JASON: It true, Star Apple. I open me mouth to sing and I ain't ever find woman who could resist.

MEDIYAH: I ain't say you lie. Regret three?

JASON: Well, I always did say when I check out, I want to have a woman 'neath me and me mouth all over she.

MEDIYAH: Eh-eh? But you got some brass!

JASON: I ain't suppose you could do tickle somethin' 'bout number three, eh?

MEDIYAH: Boy, you too bad. You does have some lawless mouth, you know.

JASON: Is me charm. Woman always find me so. Can't help it. I born that way. I makin' love to woman from me cradle. I think all that goin' now 'cause I don't even feel I have strength to do you one small rudeness. At least, you could bring you face down here and leave me have one kiss 'for I pass, nuh?

(JASON *pulls* MEDIYAH *down to him. She, far from resisting, is more than enthusiastic. At the moment of their kiss,* GRANNY ROOT *appears and gestures symbolically. Lights flash and there is thunderous sound.* GRANNY ROOT, *again, disappears.*)

JASON: Be-Jesus! Thunder and lightning and all the
element in you mouth, Woman. Me lip, me teeth, me
tongue, me throat…all aflame. I comin', God. Now,
ordinarily, when I say, "I comin'", I does mean just
that. Howsoever, I 'fraid that this time when I say,
"I comin'", I mean, "I goin'"! But, this is one terrible
damn time to pass, eh? Shite! I already see the face of
God.

MEDIYAH:
Hear me good, you altogether gorgeous thing.
I listenin' while you pretty mouth spoutin' you charm
and you pretty head restin' in the crook of me arm.
You think I 'bout to let the smallest piece of harm
come to you?
I look dumb to you?
You must be crazy in you head
if you think I goin' let you dead.

JASON: But, who you is? Bow come you here in this
beastly wood and no animal or haunt try for make
meal out you?

MEDIYAH: You notice that at last, eh? Well, I born right
here and I special.
I, Granny Root granddaughter.
I, all herb and bush and Miedo Wood water.
Is with a priestess of Science and Healin'
you dealin'.
You ain't feel, since I touch you, you fever batin'?
Whoever want to claim you life, have to keep on
    waitin',
'cause is me, Mediyah, now holdin' you fate in
she hand.
Understand?
Yes! Is me who snatch you from the mouth of Hell
and goin' make you pretty, handsome carcass well.
Close you eye and sleep, 'cause truth be to tell,
I goin' 'range meself 'bout you

and suck the venom out you.
Oh, yes man. I goin' lift
up me shift
and give you the gift
of new life.

JASON: I can't keep me eye open. I sorry. 'Bye, Gal!

MEDIYAH: Yes! Sleep on, me beauty! I goin' into the
wood and get you wood and gut string you leave
there and I goin' make you the most fine, gold quatro
you did ever see. Yes! You sleep, Mr. Sugar-Tongue, I
goin' keep you right here on this island with me 'till it
time for you to win Pecong at the Carnival. You goin
sleep all the time I ain't here, so that when I are here,
you ain't goin' have nothin' but energy...which you
goin' truly need. Oh, Man, is new life for you. In the
meantime, God, I can't wait no longer.

(MEDIYAH *throws herself, savagely, on* JASON, *who though
asleep, reacts in kind. The lights go down on them, but come
up on* GRANNY ROOT *perched in a tree and laughing eerily
and evilly.)*

GRANNY ROOT: No, m'dear. 'Taint for you to die of love
for this man or any one of they. Love? Bah!
Love does make you mind go simple
and make you face swole big with pimple.
Is hate
should motivate
a woman fate.
But, have no fear.
Granny goin' always be near
and she goin' steel you 'gainst foolishness
and approachin' bitterness.
Yes!
However, 'taint no reason why you can't have tickle
fun on the road to heartbreak and vengeance!

(GRANNY ROOT *cackles as the lights go out.)*

Scene Three

(CREON's *store.* SWEET BELLA *is behind the counter.*
FAUSTINA, *in a somewhat more sober-colored version of the*
clothes in which we last saw her, and PERSIS *enter.*)

FAUSTINA: Where you daddy?

(SWEET BELLA *indicates the back of the store.*)

FAUSTINA: Creon Pandit, you old bandit. Come out
here!

CREON: Who takin' me name in vain? (*He comes out.*)
Oh, is only Cleopatra and she hand-maiden, What you
want?

FAUSTINA: I came for me goods,

CREON: What goods? You ain't have no goods here. All
a ol' crocodile like you could have is "bads".

FAUSTINA: Don't rag with me, Man. I come to pick up
me cloth.

CREON: What cloth? You have cloth here?

FAUSTINA: Don't get me wroughted, nuh! All you know
you have cloth for me here.

CREON: You mistake. Is me, one, who have cloth here.
Is when you have some shillin' for show me, is then I
have some cloth for you. 'Till then, the cloth mine.

FAUSTINA: You ol' pirate. Is them warrin' faction in you
blood that does make you brutish so, you know. Bring
me me cloth, nuh!

CREON: Show me you money, Woman!

FAUSTINA: Here! Is three Moravian coppers. Now bring
me me cloth and I want me change!

CREON: Change? What change? You think you have
change comin'?

FAUSTINA: Don't trifle with me, you ol' fart!

CREON: I hangin' on to this cloth so long for you, you ain't think I entitle to storage charge?

FAUSTINA: Now, the man tryin' to t'ief me money. You better bring me me cloth and me change 'fore me take a torch to you and you tickle store.

CREON: Try it, Beldam. You seem to forget I also the magistrate. You just threaten the law. I could have you tail throw in jail, if I want.

FAUSTINA: Is so you would treat ol' friend, eh? No wonder you house goin' soon fall, I done read you card, you know.

CREON: You can't even read English, much less piece of card.

PERSIS: You know, you two is trial. Sometime both of you act like you don't have no brought-upsey, a-tall.

CREON: Here you damn piece of change. Next time you goin' know better. I ain't like me merchandise lay fallow on me shelf.

FAUSTINA: You talkin' chupidness. Is only two week since I order.

CREON: You too lie! The cloth have two foot dust, it there so long. I had was to wrap it so it ain't fade.

FAUSTINA: I have a good mind…

CREON: …Since when?…

FAUSTINA: …to carry me trade elsewhere and not come in here a next time. You ain't deserve me patronage.

PERSIS: And, you would please tell me, to which next establishment you would favor with you trade, since Creon Pandit store the only one 'round here?

CREON: Make she know it! Even if somebody have enough craziness to try to raise a emporia and want to rival with me, he ain't goin' be so fool as to sell goods

to you. Bella, reach me that roll of black bombazine
from the shelf and let we get this ol' crow from out me
shop.

PERSIS: Black Bombazine?

CREON: And, careful. Blow off the dust! I ain't want
you to dirty you frock.

PERSIS: Black Bombazine? You order black Bombazine?

FAUSTINA: Creon Pandit, you mouth too big. Who
authorize you to put me business on you clothesline?

CREON: You ain't tell me is secret.

PERSIS: You order black Bombazine?
Who you think you is? The Queen?

FAUSTINA: And what, pray tell me, causin' such
hilarity?

PERSIS: Oh, forgive me, nuh!
I succumb to jollity
'cause you think you quality.

FAUSTINA: I is a augurer now. I can't walk 'round here
like I ordinary.

PERSIS: Oh, God! He heart! Me heart!

FAUSTINA: Shut you fool mouth! I have to have proper
dress for Carnival when it come. You think I can make
appearance in costume, rag and bead like common
jamette? All you mere mortal can wear all them color
and be the rainbow, if you so choose, but I have
standin' and station. I have responsibility. Me life
dictate by the card, them. They probably goin' ask me
to sit on the bench and be a judge.

PERSIS: Oh, God! I goin' die and I ain't even make out
me will.

FAUSTINA: As soon as you through playin' fool, you
think you can run up this bombazine into something

that look dignify without makin' too much distress on the cloth?

PERSIS: Whoop! You hear that, Creon Pandit? She majesty goin' trust me to stitch up she coronation robe, underlin' that I am. I surprise she ain't want to chance needle and thread, sheself.

FAUSTINA: You the seamstress! I, the priestress!

PERSIS: But, you is too comical.

FAUSTINA: Creon Pandit, you have stranger comin'! No! Two! No! Three!

CREON: Who comin'?

FAUSTINA: You goin' see one just now. I ain't say no more.

PERSIS: Is Mediyah!

CREON: (Shaken) Granny Root granddaughter? What she want here?

PERSIS: I ain't know. I ain't see she for same month.

(MEDIYAH, brightly dressed, enters.)

Hello, Mediyah.

MEDIYAH: Hello, ladies. Faustina, you ain't have to hide in the back stall. I ain't feel for mischief today.

PERSIS: I never see you come in Creon Pandit store 'fore now.

MEDIYAH: You right! Hello, Creon Pandit!

CREON: What you want here? You come to cause ruction? (He takes a heavy chain with a cross on it and puts it around SWEET BELLA's neck.) Bella, go to the back! (He practically pushes SWEET BELLA out.) I ain't want no pass with you!

MEDIYAH: I goin' ignore all that! I need several piece of cloth and some other t'ing. You can take it from this tickle piece of coin.

CREON: That gold!

PERSIS: Gold?

MEDIYAH: Gold!

CREON: It real?

MEDIYAH: You could try it out on you tooth.

CREON: But, I ain't have change for this.

MEDIYAH: Who tell you I goin' need change? Is a whole lot of cloth and t'ing I needin'. Here me list! You could fill it?

CREON: Yes, Mistress. Sweet Bella, help me gather these item, them.

(SWEET BELLA *returns and helps* CREON *to gather items.*)

PERSIS: So, Mediyah, where you was all this time? Is so long I ain't see you. I does ask you brother, Cedric, for you all the time and him, that sweet-singin' boy, say he ain't know where you is. Sometime, I does pass by you house, tryin' for a glimpse, but the shutter always shut and I ain't hear you singin' inside like I always was use to.

MEDIYAH: What for you want to get in me business?

PERSIS: I ain't mean no harm.

MEDIYAH: Persis, you does make me chuckle. Don't fret youself! I decide to stay on Miedo Wood Island!

(FAUSTINA *and* PERSIS *elbow each other's ribs.* CREON *and* SWEET BELLA *look aghast.*)

MEDIYAH: I decide to build me a little castilla over there.

PERSIS: But that is one angry, tickle piece of sand in the sea. How you could live there?

MEDIYAH: Careful! Is me home you talkin' 'bout. Creon Pandit, I want them thing deliver...

CREON: I ain't have nobody so fool to go to Miedo Wood Island and I, for sure, ain't goin'...

MEDIYAH: Who ask you for do such? I ask you for do such?

CREON: But, you say...

MEDIYAH: You ain't let me finish "say". Now, I want them thing deliver to me old house. Me Granny house.

CREON: I ain't goin' there neither. Everybody know you Granny house hold badness and animosity for me and all Pandit.

MEDIYAH: How that could be so? How you could say such? Cedric there! The house ain't have no badness and animosity for he. Even though he ain't have the name, he a Pandit!

CREON: Ain't nobody 'live could prove that!

MEDIYAH: You right! Nobody 'live could prove it.

(FAUSTINA *and* PERSIS *have not stopped elbowing each other's ribs.*)

MEDIYAH: So how could the house have haunt and botheration for you if Cedric there? And you and he ... relate.

CREON: I ain't claim that!

PERSIS: But, Creon, all of we does know the whole story.

CREON: Ain't nobody know no whole story...nothin'!

PERSIS: Faustina, tell the man

FAUSTINA: Me ain't know nothin'! I does mind me business. Me lip…seal!

MEDIYAH: You grew wise since I last see you. Creon bring…

CREON: Creon don't bring! I, the owner! I, the magistrate! I don't bring nothin'. I have delivery boy for that!

MEDIYAH: Then, why you causin' such ado? Surely, me Granny house ain't have no bad spirit for you delivery boy. Unless, unbeknownst to all we, he a secret Pandit, too. Well, have them thing deliver to the porch if he ain't feel to come inside. I could, ha-ha, spirit thereto me island. I got me ways, you know. Oh, and by the way, I see that fine white-cloth suit you have in you window. Put that in with me purchase, too.

(FAUSTINA and PERSIS. *Elbows and ribs*)

CREON: But that suit is for man!

MEDIYAH: You think I blind and ain't know that?

CREON: But, you can't just buy man suit, so! You have to know size and fittin' and that suit ain't look, to me experience eye, like it goin' fit Cedric, unless you goin' alterate it.

MEDIYAH: And who, in the Heaven you know, tell you I buyin' suit for Cedric. Me brother buy he own clothin'. Ain't you or nobody else have to bother you head with worriation. The suit plenty fit for the one who goin' wear it. Now, fold and box it nice. While I thinkin', you could throw in two, three of then white trouser the same size as the suit pant. Here! I want you wind this piece of red ribbon 'round it and tie me one, big bow.

CREON: You still have change comin'.

MEDIYAH: I know that!

CREON: I ain't want you to think I cheat you.

MEDIYAH: Creon Pandit, is no way you could t'ief
me. You know that. You hold on to them coin I have
comin'. I establishin' credick. 'Bye! 'Bye, ladies.
Faustina, you could talk now and the two of you could
stop "hunchin'" one another. You rib must be black
and blue. I ain't comin' back today. I give you me
word. (*She goes and then, pops her head back in the door.*)
Of course, sometime I does lie and me word ain't mean
a t'ing. (*She laughs, raucously, then leaves.*)

FAUSTINA: Woman, you have me rib sore.

PERSIS: And you, me! You ever hear such?

FAUSTINA: You better hush you mout', Woman, and
wait 'till she get out of ear-shot!

CREON: Sweet Bella, take this coin and put it in the
coffer. You two bush-rat goin' have to vacate, 'cause I
closin' down. I think I goin pi rum up meself, lickle bit.

FAUSTINA: Don't rush me, nuh! You think she goin'
give you she patronage all the time? Bah! You got a
next think comin'!

PERSIS: That gold part of Granny Root legendary
fortune, come what you bet! But I wonder who them
suit and pant for?

FAUSTINA: Come what you bet, then for the same
mysterious person plant then two alligator pear seed in
she belly.

PERSIS: What you say? what you say?

FAUSTINA: You ain't see, eh? Well, of course, you ain't
have the power of foresight and divination. You ain't
have the gift and you ain't have the card. She carryin'
two piece of something in there. Ain't I say is three
stranger comin' to Creon Pandit shop?

CREON: Is so you did say!

FAUSTINA: So? She is the one stranger, for she never set she foot in here before. And she carryin' two in she oven. One and two does always come out...three...if I does know my mathematic.

PERSIS: I thought she did look sorta...different... But, no! You pickin' leaf from the wrong bush, Woman.

CREON: She look the same to me. Lickle cleaner, maybe, but... Oh, you ol' man-eater, you. How you a-know so much?

FAUSTINA: You forget me card?

CREON: Oh, yes. I does forget you is the all-seein' Oracle, Well, you could tell me, Sybil, who she lay up with?

PERSIS: Yes! That what I want to know. Better still, who lay up with she?

FAUSTINA: How I should know?

CREON: I thought you could read so much card.

FAUSTINA: Is card tell me she carryin'.

PERSIS: Then, card should tell you who she carryin' for.

CREON: I surprise such a monumental occurrence, like who pumpin' pipe and tool to Mediyah, escape you eye. Well, it look like the two you goin' have to trilly over to Miedo Wood Island if you want find out. Shark won't molest you if you swim. They scare. You two is the only other two I know could go there and come back without all them haunt and animal and t'ing bother then. They know you is they relative. Get outta here now. I tell you I closin' me shop!

FAUSTINA: We goin', you brute!

PERSIS: You too rude. 'Bye, Sweet Bella. Is a shame you can't speak, but is you father disposition that get the curse put on you.

CREON: *(Most angry.)* Get out, you two ol' harridan!

(FAUSTINA and PERSIS go. SWEET BELLA regards CREON.)

CREON: Sweet Bella, you mustn't mind what them
say. Both of them is bitter, bitter woman. They soul
sour with invective and vinegar. Don't look so at you
daddy. You daddy love only you and you mother, rest
she soul. I never play ram on she. I marry she and I
stay in faith 'till she pass. Sure, I do plenty thing 'fore
I marry, but I suppose to, I, man and when I young, I
had was to run with the wind and be wild thing. You
think I handsome now? God, you should see me then.
When me hair was thicker and blacker than a night
without moon. I was a sheik. I could teach any damn
Casanova a thing or two, believe me. Then, one day, I
see this black, black girl. She hair…short and tight.. like
a clench fist. She lip like it 'bout to bust with too much
honey and she voice like a breeze. She eye burn hole
right through me. She skin? Ah, she skin. She skin was
a miracle of black velvet with the sun shinin' behind
it. I never see nothin' like that. I completely bewitch by
she and she skin. That same skin I couldn't bring to me
father table. Ah, girl. You ain't understand. I ain't make
the world. T'ing is t'ing and I ain't set that rule. I was
important. I was Mighty, Royal Most Perfect, Grand
King Calabash. I did win Pecong five time consecutive.
Only man ever do that is me daddy. I was important.
The girl was…black!

*(SWEET BELLA looks at CREON. The veiled figure of
GRANNY ROOT passes, silently, through the room, They
both shudder, as if a cold wind had passed over them.)*

CREON: Still, I would rather you had all the black
blood in the world, if I could just hear you voice say,
"Daddy, I love you." I know that ol' woman curse me
when she daughter pitch sheself off Devil Cliff. She
deliver twin and then she pitch sheself into the wind.

She body never find in the water. She mother swear sheself against me line from there on out. You came out without voice. I do it to you and I too, too sorry. I love you so, but you is me only regret. Oh, Sweet Bella, I was young and I ain't had better sense than to be young. Oh, now. Go fetch one of them lickle black boy from the back and tell he he have delivery to make.

(SWEET BELLA *starts to go.*)

CREON: No! Wait! On second thought, I think I goin' take this one over meself.

(SWEET BELLA *looks, understandingly, at her father.*)

(PERSIS *comes back in, calling to the off-stage* FAUSTINA.)

PERSIS: Just wait there! Ain't no need for you for came in. I sure I leave me purse on the counter. Creon?

CREON: I close!

PERSIS: Oh, shut up, Man. Here ten shillin'. Put me 'side ten yard of them black Bombazine and I pick it up when I come in next time. And, hear me! Nobody say you have to be town-crier and put me business in the ear of all and sundry creation. You follow?
(She goes, calling to the off-stage FAUSTINA.)
I find it! I told you, ain't I?

FAUSTINA: Oh, you find it where it drop on the floor?

PERSIS: How you know it drop on the floor, dear Sister?

FAUSTINA: I read it in the card, Poopsie! The card make me see all thing.

(CREON *and* SWEET BELLA *smile at each other as he locks the door of his shop.*)

(*Lights*)

Scene Four

(The old hut. CEDRIC *is sprawled, drunkenly, on the floor. Jugs, bottles, wooden wine cups and other things indicate there have been many lengthy parties going on.* CEDRIC's *two dancing girls are sprawled, inelegantly, on either side of him.* MEDIYAH, *followed by the ever-present* GRANNY ROOT, *enters. Both are horrified at what they see.* GRANNY ROOT *picks up an old besom and starts after* CEDRIC, *but* MEDIYAH *wrests the broom from her hands before she can strike.)*

GRANNY ROOT: The place look just like ram and she-goat live here.

MEDIYAH: Don't wrought youself. I goin' take care of this. *(Broom in hand, she stands over the sleepers. She doesn't speak loudly.)* You two courtesan, wake you worthless tail up!

(The two girls stir, drowsily.)

MEDIYAH: Wake up, you good-for-nothin' but good-time wenches!

(The two wake with a start and are about to scream, but a gesture from MEDIYAH *silences them.)*

MEDIYAH: Not a sound. Vacate these premise 'fore I take this besom and sweep you into eternity. Make haste!

(The two quickly gather their things and, terrified and trying to scream, run from the hut.)

GRANNY ROOT: You do good, Girl. You does bring such joy and laughter to me spirit. Come what you bet, if than have on undergarment, they soil them.

MEDIYAH: Cedric!

*(*MEDIYAH *pitches the contents of a water pitcher in* CEDRIC's *face. Sputtering, he lashes out, blindly, with his cutlass.)*

CEDRIC: Aaiieeee! I goin' kill...

MEDIYAH: Get up!

CEDRIC: You brain come loose? Why for you pitch water at me for?

GRANNY ROOT: Criminal!

MEDIYAH: 'Cause you ain't wake when I call you name!

CEDRIC: Tyrant! You crazy?

MEDIYAH: Look how you does have this place. Pig does live cleaner than this.

GRANNY ROOT: Like you ain't have the first bit of brought-upsy!

CEDRIC: Who fault that? Where you was all this time?

MEDIYAH: What you say?

CEDRIC: Is well over three, four month since you set foot in here.

MEDIYAH: So?

CEDRIC: So, so don't bring you errant self in here complainin' 'bout the place look like pig sty, if you ain't here to clean it!

GRANNY ROOT: What gall!

MEDIYAH: But, you is a ol' bitch, you know that? What you think I does be? Maid servant and you the king? You too fool. You waitin' all this time for me to do you service?

CEDRIC: Who else? I, the man here!

MEDIYAH: Hear him, nuh! 'Cause he have something dangle 'tween he leg, him can't pass broom 'cross the floor. I should kick you in you vital and make you stone inoperative.

GRANNY ROOT: Blackguard!

MEDIYAH Since you does so need woman to pick up
behind you, why you ain't make them two wilted
blossom I just chase from here do such, eh? How them
could lay up here cross you and you smellin' so foul?
This a island with water on all side. Ain't no reason for
man to smell worse than ram-goat in summer.

CEDRIC: You better hush you mouth 'fore I vex and tell
me where you was all this time.

MEDIYAH: On Miedo Wood Island. Why you eye open
so agape? That place ain't hold no fear for me.

CEDRIC: I know that. Is only that is 'bout this same
Miedo Wood Island and you I been thinkin'. I need you
to go and axe me off piece wood from the Calabash
tree. I need a next quatro.

MEDIYAH: What do you old one?

CEDRIC: It mash up! Me and me compay, them, saunter
into Creon Pandit cantina for some merriment and
libation and we sittin' there mindin' all we own
business, when this bunch of bum…say them from
Tougou Island…come at we to issue challenge for
Pecong at Carnival. Tell me them have some dilly with
voice and brain better than me and him goin' cause me
to fall in the contest. Of course, I accept the challenge
'cause no way me and me magic quatro could lose.
Well, that devil-grog that Creon Pandit does sell in he
place is the cause of it all. 'Fore you know it, one thing
does lead to a next and one of them Tougou-boy, full of
drunk, sayin' some nastiness 'bout me ancestry.

MEDIYAH: Eh-eh?

GRANNY ROOT: I hope you kill he…

CEDRIC: …and I had was to grab he by he collar and
butt he…

GRANNY ROOT: Good!

CEDRIC: ...and before you know it, he boy, them, jump in and we havin' one grand punch-up in the place...

GRANNY ROOT: I hope you wreck Creon Pandit cantina.

CEDRIC: ...and we havin' fun, fun, fun! Then one of them devil get lucky and catch me a vicious blow back me neck and I fall quite on top me quatro. It turn serious then. I ain't utter a word. I get up. Is the first time I ever knock off me feet you know, and I evil now. I pick up what use to be me quatro and look at it. It mash flat. It like it collapse. The ruction stop and you could cut the silence, it so thick. I look at me compay, them. Them lookin' at me. A look pass 'tween we that tell them is all me fight now. Them Tougou boy ain't know what happenin'! Suddenly, without warnin', I scream and spring like cat and pitch meself 'mong then. Me arm and cutlass flailin' like windmill. You ain't see hurricane do more damage than me. -Most of them run, but they is two who ain't goin' mush nobody on quatro no more. I tell you, I was so full up, I had was to grab both then sweet, brown gal you chase 'way and wear them out at the same time. Anyway I need you to bring me some wood from Miedo and I could fashion me a next quatro in time for Carnival. Is just enough time for the wood to cure proper and I could use the same string so you ain't have to kill cat for me.

MEDIYAH: I can't do that, Cedric.

CEDRIC: What you say?

GRANNY ROOT: She say true!

MEDIYAH: I say I can't do that. Brother, is only one time I could get wood for each person from !Miedo. You done have you share.

CEDRIC: You sayin' you can't get no more wood?

MEDIYAH: I could get plenty wood, but no more for you. Is one time only for each person.

CEDRIC: Bat, you could do it. You special. We special.
We born there.

MEDIYAH: No! Is only me born there. You forget. You
born in the boat on the way. Is only after we land and
Granny bring Mother ashore that I came out.

CEDRIC: It ain't matter. You have the power.

MEDIYAH: But if I break the law of Science, I lose me
power.

CEDRIC: So, you ain't goin' help me? You twin brother?
You desert me, eh?

MEDIYAH: You desert youself.

CEDRIC: Okay, Sister. I ain't goin' beg! No need to
worry you head. You brother still have he voice. Be still
have he brain. He could still sing Calypso and shout
Pecong better when he drunk and sick than any foot-
jam who sober. I ain't need you or you quatro tree for
help me.

MEDIYAH: Where you goin', Brother?

CEDRIC: 'Taint none you damn business, but I goin'
to join me friend, them. Is one thing I did alway say,
"When you family ain't stand by you, you alway have
friend." I come into this world. I ain't ask, mind you,
and ain't nobody ask me, but I come. The first thing
they tell me is I ain't have me Daddy name and me
Mother kill sheself. Then me Granny kick out and now,
I ain't even have a sister. Well, thank be to God, I have
friend who love me and would buy me a cup of grog
when I feelin' low. I ain't have no family would do so.
(He goes.)

MEDIYAH: Cedric!

GRANNY ROOT: You can't stop him. T'ing is t'ing and
they can't change. Everything charted and goin' 'long.
It all plan by greater than we.

MEDIYAH: Granny, I ain't feel too sorry for Cedric. How come that does be so? After all, he and I is twin. I should be feel somethin' more than I does feel?

GRANNY ROOT: I already tell you. T'ing is t'ing. That is all.

MEDIYAH: Okay, Granny.

GRANNY ROOT: Now, on this particular matter, I ain't interfere before...but I think...when you get back to the island and wake Jason Allcock from he induce slumber, you better tell he that he goin' be daddy to you twin you carryin' in you belly.

MEDIYAH: You know, eh? You ain't say nothin' so I thought I had put one over on you.

GRANNY ROOT: Oh, Child, I tired tellin' you...

GRANNY ROOT & MEDIYAH: ..."Granny see everything! Granny know everything! Granny goin' alway be here..."

MEDIYAH: ...Yes, Granny, I know. I goin' tell him today. I think is time. But, first, make I clean up this place tickle bit.

GRANNY ROOT: Leave it! Cedric ain't goin' need this place a next time. You ain't goin' have no more use for it.

(From off-stage, CREON calls.)

CREON: Hola! Bola! Who in there?

GRANNY ROOT: Himself!

MEDIYAH: What you want, Creon Pandit?

CREON: I bring all them thing you purchase. I transfer them to you boat already and I goin'.

MEDIYAH: Wait!

(MEDIYAH goes out to CREON who seems rooted to his spot.)

CREON: What you want?

MEDIYAH: My brother and some boy, them, have a tumble and bruck up you cantina?

CREON: Yes!

MEDIYAH: Why you ain't say nothin'?

CREON: You brother sittin' there mindin' he business, when them Tougou-rascal come in and start botheration. Well, I a Calabash. The only one 'live to claim such and it look like Cedric goin' soon join me in me advance state. I ain't like it the way them fellow come in and make challenge and...

MEDIYAH: And?

CREON: Them say something they ain't have no cause to say. Cedric well within he right to knock them over.

(MEDIYAH *takes some coins from her pocket.*)

MEDIYAH: Here!

CREON: What this for?

MEDIYAH: Damage!

CREON: But...

MEDIYAH: I ain't want no child of me mother to owe a thing to you.

GRANNY ROOT: You do well, Granddaughter

CREON: You ain't have to do this...

MEDIYAH: We get this far without you help and we ain't need it now.

(CREON *backs away, cautiously, but hides behind a tree. Of course, he can only see* MEDIYAH *as she kneels on the ground and bends her body in supplication.* GRANNY ROOT *puts her hands on* MEDIYAH's *shoulders and stops her movement.*)

GRANNY ROOT: Creon Pandit watchin'!

MEDIYAH: I know!

GRANNY ROOT: Then, let he see. 'Bye, old hut! We ain't need you no more.

(GRANNY ROOT, *her hands on* MEDIYAH's *shoulders, as if passing power into her, looks upward.* MEDIYAH *thrusts her arms out and the hut "bursts into flame".* CREON, *in terror, runs from the scene. Lights.*)

Scene Five

(*The hut of* JASON *and* MEDIYAH *on Miedo Wood Island.* JASON, *surrounded by flowers and baskets of tropical fruit, sleeps soundly and blissfully.* MEDIYAH, *the beribboned suit-box in her arms and followed by* GRANNY ROOT, *enters.*)

MEDIYAH: Each time I does look at that man, I does want to jump he.

GRANNY ROOT: Be quite pretty.

MEDIYAH: All over and all the time.
In the sun or in the night,
He pretty by day or candlelight.

GRANNY ROOT: And you body all a-jumble
when him act all rough and tumble.
Even when him claw and clutch you
It still feel soft where him touch you.

MEDIYAH: I know you does alway say you does live through me, but you could feel he, for true?

GRANNY ROOT: He know how to make woman say, "Wuppi-wuppi!". He know he art. He a skill practitioner and if you ain't careful and hold youself… just so…you could lose you power as well as you heart. It time to wake he and tell he you news. I goin' off on some revel.

(GRANNY ROOT *disappears.* MEDIYAH *approaches the sleeping* JASON, *taking a small vial from her neck and a leaf from her pocket. She puts the vial to his lips and after emptying it of its contents, passes the leaf over his face. He stretches, yawns and wakes.)*

JASON: Hi, Gal. Make you drop you shift and get in this bed so I could do you. Then I want me sayuno and after I eat, I goin' do you a next time. I feelin' like a bull-ram today and I ravenous for everything in me sight. Bring you face down here and let me attack it.

MEDIYAH: Man, how come we ain't lash up 'fore this time?

JASON: Be thankful for "now", Gal. Don't have regret for the past. Is that same "past" does lead us to this same "now".

MEDIYAH: Well, Philosopher, I have tickle piece news for you. I know for long time now, but I happy with me news…so I keep it to meself,

JASON: Eh-eh? I hear this tone million time already. You knock up?

MEDIYAH: Bow you does know?

JASON: You think I does born yesterday? Ain't I tell you plenty gal in Tougou make baby for me?

MEDIYAH: I remember is so you say, but none of then wench give you boy like I goin' give you.

JASON: I hear that before, too!

MEDIYAH: This time, it true.

JASON: How you know?

MEDIYAH: Jason, look me in me eye! You does know me to lie? You ain't know, by now, I special? I real special! When I find you, you body all chew up and mew up and have scar and t'ing. Where them scar now? You see them? When I find you, you ain't think

you goin' see the next day, you body weak so and
creak so. Since that time, you does feel one ache? You
ain't been nothin' but young and strong and givin' me
body all the pleasure with you youth and you strength.
You ain't even have a memory of how tear up and sear
up you was when I first see you. When I leave off from
you, I does go 'bout me business here and elsewhere.
With all the wild animal they does have here. any
does come to give you aggravation? No! I does put up
barrier that no haunt, spirit or wild t'ing could breach.
You belong to me, Jason Allcock, and nothin' goin'
change that. I put charm all over you. So when I tell
you, you goin' have son, believe it. And when I tell
you, you goin' have two son, you better believe that
too…for it too true.

JASON: You tellin' me I goin' have twin boy?

MEDIYAH: I, yet, goin' convince you of me power. You
feelin' young and strong?

JASON: Yes!

MEDIYAH: You feel for give me tickle tumble?

JASON: All the time!

MEDIYAH: You feel for make me body sing with you
music?

JASON: Like you the quatro and I the picker!

MEDIYAH: You feel for make you mouth run rampant
all over me terrain?

JASON: Woman, you have me hotter than Satan fire!
Bring youself over to me. Let me have at you.

MEDIYAH: No, Doux-doux.
You come over here and get me.
Come over here and let me
give you all the love
and fulfillment of

all you dream
and treasure.
Come over here and take me.
Came over here and make me
tingle with delight.
Make me fill you night
with sweet scream
and murmur of pleasure.
Come! Come! Come, sweet man!
Come! Come get me, if you can!

(JASON *struggles, but can't seem to rise from the bed.*)

JASON: What happenin'? I can't move! What you do to me?

MEDIYAH: You know how you does enter
me center
and bury youself to you hilt
while all the tine you croonin' lilt
and drippin' sugar word in me ear?
Them word does sometime cause me eye to tear.
Them alway cause me heart to flame,
Well, try to lullaby me now!
I bet all
you can call
is me name.

JASON: Mediyah, mediyah mediyah mediyah! Mediyah, mediyah mediyah mediyah, mediyah?

(JASON, *suddenly angry, calms himself and looks, coolly at* MEDIYAH.)

MEDIYAH: So you must believe me when I tell you that I carryin' two boy for you...right here in this belly. You tell me about all them silly, flirty t'ing who make baby for you. Well, I ain't like them and them ain't like I! I the most different woman you goin' meet. No other like me. I givin' you boy 'cause you say you want them. Jason, I give you anything you want.

GRANNY ROOT: Mediyah?

MEDIYAH: You want to be Grand King Calabash and I goin' see to it. All you have to do is ask

GRANNY ROOT: Mediyah?

JASON: You mighty impressive, but you ain't know me. Plenty woman does love me. Why? Them know I wayward and never goin' make they legal. Them know, too, that I good to all me daughter. Every one me daughter have me love and me name and the first straight-leg rogue who even look like them came to do they badness with him stone in him hand, have me machete where him leg meet. I a rascal, but I honest and I ain't want nothin' from nobody I ain't work for, meself. When you find me in this same wood, all mash up and slash up, I ask you for anything except youself for me to kiss and do a little smooch? No! And you could refuse me, you know! I ain't beg! I ask you to heal me and seal me and do all this kindness? No! I come here with me machete in me hand and I prepare to do me own battle or die! Is me way! I make me own way and me own fate! Is me strip me wood from Calabash tree! Is me strangle wild cat and pull out she gut. Is you make up me quatro, true, but I ask you to do that? No! So, is me who take it 'part and make it up a next time…my way! And, be-Christ, is me who goin, win Pecong and t'ing by meself! On me own! Now, I ain't ungrateful. I too glad you find me and mind me and sure me and sure me and love me and carryin' two boy for me. But I rather you take them two boy and yank they out you belly. I rather be all scar up and mar up. I rather you let all me blood run out and get drink up by the earth. I rather you leave me die, than deny me the right to win the contest on me own. I ain't need magic! I ain't need conjure! I ain't need sorcery! I only need me! Me! Me! Me! Now, if you want to spout incantation and work spell and do me badness and

sadness and evilness, go to it. I came into this world
a honest man and I go out the same. I ain't scare of a
livin' arse…excuse me language…in this world, so do
you worse!

MEDIYAH: Jason, you make me love you…too much.

GRANNY ROOT: *(From afar)* Mediyah!

MEDIYAH: I ain't want to be nothin' but the only
woman in you life!

GRANNY ROOT: *(From afar)* Mediyah!

MEDIYAH: I ain't care for be nothin' but she who have
you all the time!

GRANNY ROOT: Mediyah!

MEDIYAH: Tell me, Jason! Say it! Tell me you ain't love
nobody but you Mediyah and I do anything you tell
me. Anything you say! Anything you ask! The world
goin' belong to you if you say you love me the same
like I love you. I use me power to give you anything!
Everything!

*(GRANNY ROOT appears. Lights flash. MEDIYAH and
JASON freeze.)*

GRANNY ROOT: Mediyah, you ain't have no power.
You just give it to this man. He hold power over you,
now. You surrender to he. You just a ordinary woman,
now. You goin' have to leave this island. Granny goin'
see you out safely, but you must go. Both you and he.
You can't protect he no more. You can't make he sleep
with secret potion and t'ing. You goin' have to go 'fore
cockcrow or you doom. Obey me!

(GRANNY ROOT gestures. MEDIYAH moves.)

MEDIYAH: Granny, what happen? I ain't know a feelin'
like this before. I burnin' up. Me stomach all a-churn.

GRANNY ROOT: You fall too much in love. That is all.
You lose control.

MEDIYAH: I ain't like it. It hurt. It like a million jamette dancin' Carnival and trampin' in we head. Me body feel like Damballah, heself, pitchin' rock and flame at me.

GRANNY ROOT: I did almost know that feelin' once. Long time ago…but I check it! I see the way of the world and I say, "No!"

MEDIYAH: Take it away, Granny! Take away this feelin'!

GRANNY ROOT: Is only you can do such.

MEDIYAH: How? Tell me how! I do it right now!

GRANNY ROOT: Remove the man!

MEDIYAH: What?

GRANNY ROOT: Banish he from you heart! Call down thunder and lightnin' to strike he from here! Cast he into the pit! 'Cause flame to rise up 'round he and incinerate he! Use Science! Use skill! Kill he!

(MEDIYAH, *aroused by* GRANNY ROOT's *fervor, gestures wildly. Nothing happens to* JASON.)

MEDIYAH: Nothin' ain't happen!

GRANNY ROOT: 'Cause you ain't want it to. In you heart, you ain't want it to.

(MEDIYAH *gestures again, falls to her knees in prayer, dances wildly, prostrates herself, does all manner of things, but nothing happens.*)

GRANNY ROOT: Is like I say, Darlin', you too much in love. A woman, too much in love, ain't have no power! Now, you have to prepare to leave here. I can give you only to cockcrow. Then you must follow me close or you mighty love goin' be you miserable death!

(MEDIYAH *sinks to the ground, sobbing.*)

GRANNY ROOT: Poor, ordinary woman!

(GRANNY ROOT *disappears as* JASON *returns to normal.*)

JASON: No! I can't say them word you want, 'cause I
ain't feel to say such. I ain't tell lie to you or no other
woman. I ain't find she yet who could make me feel
and say them word. When I find she, I goin' know it.
When I find she, I goin' feel it. When I find she, I goin'
be proud to say it. I truly fond of you. For true, no gal
ever treat me so good like you, but more than this, I
can't say. Bring me boy, them, safe to this world. and
I give you honor and paradise. Now on them term,
you want me, still? Tell me now. We could fall down
on the grass, this night, and see Heaven. We could
know beauty and bliss like we never know, for I feelin'
young and strong and a little extra of me juice good
for them two boy you have in there! We could...eh-eh?
What do you? Why you a-cry?

MEDIYAH: Jason, we have to leave this place before
cockcrow!

JASON: Why? You no more happy here?

MEDIYAH: Listen!

(*Almost inaudibly, we can hear animal sounds and horrible
noises. They grow louder and louder.* JASON *picks up his
weapon as* MEDIYAH *clings to him for protection.*)

MEDIYAH: I scare. I can't protect we no more. We must
leave this place.

JASON: Before cockcrow, you say?

MEDIYAH: Yes, Darlin'.

JASON: Then we still have lickle time.

MEDIYAH: We should go now.

JASON: Before cockcrow, Doux-doux. We have time.
I goin' make all them tear
distappear.
I goin' whisper rudeness in you ear.

MEDIYAH: We ain't have time.

JASON: Two spice bun bakin' in you oven.
It take time.
Just like you and me
out to do some lovin'
it take time.
We can't go rush and reelin'.
It don't pay goin' fast
if you want the feelin'
to last.
You and me
havin' lickle funnin'.
It take time.
Then we flee
'fore we let the sun in,
but it take time.
So, lay back now
and I will sing you flower,
cover you with kiss
'till the mornin' hour,
touch you with me hand
(*is only me hand reach you*)
sing honey in you ear
that way I will teach you
the meaning of the word,
a word you've only heard,
"Sublime"
But, it take time.

(*They fall to the ground, oblivious to the once again, rising
sounds of animals and jungle horrors.* GRANNY ROOT
appears, the noises fade gradually and JASON *and* MEDIYAH
are in embrace. MEDIYAH, *still apprehensive, tries to urge
him out of the wood.*)

JASON: Slow, slow, slow!
I ain't use to runnin'.
I take time.

Time to show
me cleverness and cunnin'.
Take we time.
So, lay back now,
precious little flower.
Lay back now.
Only I does have the power
to ease you every fear.
Nothin' here goin' haunt you.
Even ghost can see
just how bad me want you.
We can beat this jungle.
Ain't no mountain we can't climb.
But, it take time.

(GRANNY ROOT *trails her veil over the prone pair.*)

GRANNY ROOT: All thing take time, but time goin' soon done!

(GRANNY ROOT *disappears.*)

JASON: Slow, Sweetness. Cockrow a long way off. We ain't have no rush. We just go easy.

(MEDIYAH *surrenders…completely.*)

END OF ACT ONE

ACT TWO

Scene One

(Months later. The hut of MEDIYAH *built on the site of the old one. It is overgrown with vines and weeds. Inside,* MEDIYAH *sits in and old rocking chair. Very much pregnant, it's obvious she's not cleaned the place in a while. Outside,* PERSIS *and* FAUSTINA *approach furtively, They wait until they are directly within hearing distance, elbow each other in the ribs and, gleefully and deliberately, speak aloud.)*

FAUSTINA: Persis?

PERSIS: What is it, Faustina?

FAUSTINA: Is a lovely day for Carnival, ain't it?

PERSIS: Oh, Darlin' Sister. True. It quite lovely. And this one goin' be so special, too. That drunken Cedric goin' for he number five win.

FAUSTINA: It look like he goin' take all the prize and t'ing.

PERSIS: But, wait! Sometime ago, you did tell we that you card say ain't no triumph for Cedric this time. What happen? You did read them wrong?

FAUSTINA: As mare does find new he-horse,
so hart does find new hind
As wind does find new chart to course,
so card does change them mind.

PERSIS: You mighty prophetic and profound this mornin'. Yes, I sure goin' to this one set of Carnival. Me wouldn't miss it.

FAUSTINA: He too, neither. I wish everybody could go, but some people can't go 'cause then too shame to show then face.

PERSIS: Oh? You could tell me why?

FAUSTINA: Plenty people have plenty reason. Some shame 'cause them belly big, big, big and then ain't have man to give they legality, properness, standin' or he name.

PERSIS: You does say true? Such people does exist? No! You ain't mean it. You can't know such sinful people. You ain't raise to know such.

FAUSTINA: Me card bring me in contact with all kind. High and low.
Up and down.
Fast and slow.
Square and roun'.

PERSIS: You ain't say.

FAUSTINA: Oh, yes. I does know some people so shame 'cause them once so high and mighty and laud and lord theyself all over the place like peacock, but now them topple. Them drab like peahen and them hiney bare like pickney.

PERSIS: Oh, miseration. It too sad to see somebody once them think them empress and now, then ain't even have chamber pot. That how the world go. One day, you a good morsel. The next, you nothin' but somebody fecal deposit.

FAUSTINA: But, wait. We so busy chattin' and feelin' sorry for them what come low like snake, we ain't realize we passin' Mediyah hut.

PERSIS: No! You wrong, Sister, dearest. This ain't
Mediyah hut. At least, it ain't die hut of the Mediyah
I does know, for this place have weed all grow up on
she. The Mediyah I does know does keen she place.
She does trim she grass and have lovely flower all red
and yellow and white and t'ing. This place does look
wild like somebody what ain't have man to love they.
No! You truly wrong! This place ain't belong to our
Mediyah!

FAUSTINA: No! It belong to she! Oop! We ain't stop
to think. Maybe she does sick and can't pick up after
sheself and that why she estate look so wild and
tempest.

PERSIS: Let we go in and see after she.

(MEDIYAH, *broom in hand, comes to the door.*)

MEDIYAH: The first, ol', never-use, dry-up tart put she
foot through me portal without me permiso, I goin'
take this one besom and t'ump she into the future.

PERSIS: Oh, look, Faustina. Is Mediyah. I glad to see you
on you feet. We thought you did sick. You goin' see
you brother go for the crown tonight?

MEDIYAH: You two ol' fart better vacate me premise,
'fore I cleave you head.

FAUSTINA: You does have to humor she, Sister. You
does get quite prickly when you carryin' baby for
invisible man.

MEDIYAH: Bow you does know? The two of you barren
like a ol', empty tortoise shell.

FAUSTINA: We does forgive you you outburst, 'cause
we know it hard when woman does have to bring forth
she tickle, nameless offspring and she ain't have man.

MEDIYAH: You could look at me and say I ain't have
man? Is only you two ol' ghost could make baby from

spirit! The first fool fellow try to fit he flaccid fiber 'neath them frowsy frock to fondle and feel you fallow, infertile, infecund, faded fruit does faint from foul and fetid fragrance of you flatulence. I should long ago turn you into the serpent you is, but I 'fraid mongoose would bite you and die from you venom. Get off me place 'fore me choke you.

FAUSTINA: Come, Persis. The woman demented. We can't help she. Them devil plant in she belly by she phantom lover done drive she insane.

(MEDIYAH *disappears into her hut.*)

PERSIS: Somethin' tell me all we better haul arse.

(MEDIYAH *returns, holding something behind her back.*)

MEDIYAH: All you say I ain't have chamber pot? I not only have pochamb, but it decorate…inside and out. Here!

(MEDIYAH *flings a flowered and filled "pochamb" at then. It misses then as they flee.*)

PERSIS: (*From a safe distance*) The woman crazy and she content…foul.

FAUSTINA: Is a good thing I ain't have on me Bombazine. She would soil it if she did connect. But she aim as good as she name and all we know she ain't have that.

(GRANNY ROOT *appears and gestures at the departed duo. They scream.*)

PERSIS: Oh, God! Abomination!

FAUSTINA: The bitch must have two pochamb!!!

FAUSTINA & PERSIS: Aaaiiieee!!!

(GRANNY ROOT *goes into the hut.*)

GRANNY ROOT: It do me heart good to see them two dry whore so dirty. Look this place, nuh? Everything all awry. How you could stay in such disarray?

MEDIYAH: I ain't feel to clean. I have too much burden here.

GRANNY ROOT: Other woman does carry and still keep she place, How you could expect somebody to see you house so filthy? What this in the pot?

MEDIYAH: Lanty-pea soup. Jason tell me he comin' today, 'cause it the beginnin' of Carnival. The contest, later, you know.

GRANNY ROOT: You expect the man to eat in so filthy a confine? You soup smell good, but if I was 'live, I wouldn't eat it. You know what them always say.
"Dirty kitchen, dirty pot!
Dirty woman, dirty lot!"

MEDIYAH: Don't scold me, nuh! This place too much for me. This belly too much for me. I want to have these baby and done. I tired carryin'. I can't do nothin', I so tire. Me foot all swole up so, me can't take four step without I have agony. The sun shine and I weepy. It rain and I worse. Jason only does come once in a blue moon and when him come, him only stay lickle piece of time. Be ain't have no talk for me. He ain't touch me and is him do this thing to me, you know. He ain't look at me. He only say him want to know how him two son comin' 'long. Be come late…when it dark…and he gone 'fore mornin'. After all this t'ing over, I goin' rip out me tube. I ain't goin' through this a next time. Never!

GRANNY ROOT: Such a much complaint.

MEDIYAH: Granny, I miserable! And, oh, God…them kick me again! Bow baby not even born could do they mother such cruelty?

GRANNY ROOT: You is a ordinary woman. You havin' ordinary pain. You makin' ordinary complaint. The magic gone, Child. Havin' baby is most real! Jason comin'. I goin'!

(GRANNY ROOT *disappears.* JASON *enters.*)

MEDIYAH: Hello, Darlin'.

JASON: This place filthy! I can't stay here! How you feel? Me two son alright?

MEDIYAH: They fine and kickin'. I make lanty-pea soup for you.

JASON: You ain't expect me to eat nothin' from this place? How I know you pot clean?

MEDIYAH: I make the soup for good luck!

JASON: I ain't need no soup for win!

MEDIYAH: I know, but don't rush off. Plenty time 'fore the festivities, them.

JASON I can't find place to stretch out or sit. I goin'! After I win, I might could come back and let you peek at me trophy, but you better pick up this place…else I not settin' foot in here. Me mother ain't raise me in no dirty house and I ain't want me son raise in no dirty house. You goin' wish me, "Bon Chance"?

MEDIYAH: Yes. I gettin' up just now.

(MEDIYAH *rises and offers her lips for* JASON *to kiss. He offers his cheek. She kisses it.*)

JASON: Careful! Don't dirty me suit. Why you don't go to the pond beneath Yama Fall and have a dip and cleanse youself, At least, woman, you could fill a basin and drop a rag in it and then pass it over you body. I ain't like no unclean woman. I ain't like no unclean woman for the mother of me son. I have to go. 'Bye!

(JASON *leaves.* MEDIYAH, *abject and sobbing, sinks to the ground.* GRANNY ROOT *appears.*)

GRANNY ROOT: Ordinary woman! Ordinary woman!
Ordinary woman!
Ordinary woman,
less than whole.
Give 'way she brain,
she heart, she soul.
Now, she playin'
ordinary role.
All because
she lose control.
Ordinary woman
feelin' sad.
Ordinary woman
feelin' bad.
Ordinary woman
soon get mad.
Then, ordinary woman
once more, glad!

MEDIYAH: Granny, you did say somethin'?

GRANNY ROOT: No, Darlin'. Granny ain't say nothin'
a-tall.

(*Lights*)

Scene Two

(*Carnival! Music! Dancing' The townsfolk…masked and colorfully costumed!* CREON, *resplendent in gold, a blue ribbon of honor across his chest, a silver and gold cape, bejeweled cane and a crown on his head, leads the revelers.* SWEET BELLA, *costumed as a radiant Cleopatra, dances with some of the men.* FAUSTINA, *in her somber Bombazine dress, enters regally with the air of a great lady dispensing alms to the poor, Her dress is betrayed, however, by the many gauzy,*

*fiery yellow and red petticoats that peek from beneath the
hen of her dress.* PERSIS, *enters in a more joyous manner.
Her costume features more gauzy orange and red petticoats
than that of her sister. Her parasol is trimmed with the same
material.* FAUSTINA *turns her nose up at her sister and
dances, sedately.* PERSIS, *riant, is having the time of her life.
As* CREON *passes the sisters, he uses his cane to lift their
skirts.)*

CREON: Mornin', Ladies. I always did think all you
have secret fire 'neath you skirt, them.

(FAUSTINA *"objects", but* PERSIS *lifts her skirt even higher
to show more,* CREON *laughs and whoops. Everyone swirls
around a slightly elevated square festooned with gaily-
colored bunting, giving it the look of a boxing ring.* CEDRIC,
*in his Chanticleer costume, pompously enters with his
entourage. They parade, ceremoniously, as* CEDRIC *steps
into the "ring". He spars, much in the manner of a boxer.)*

PERSIS: Well, it look like you card finally make up them
mind. Cedric done vanquish all he foe. Is only one final
mystery challenger to go.

FAUSTINA: Ain't I tell you, Miss? The card, them, don't
lie. Them ain't like same people I does know, who
when you does turn you back, does make them dress
out of all me extra piece of black Bombazine.

PERSIS: Oh, hush you mouth. Is me own black
Bombazine. You think you is the only one could call
sheself, "Lady"?

FAUSTINA: "Lady" t'ief!

(*Suddenly, there is a hush. The music and the hubbub stop.
The crowd parts and,* JASON, *clad in a black, figure-revealing
costume topped by a close-fitting, black hood with the horns
of a ram and wearing a black mask, appears...golden quatro
in his hands. He walks, silently, around the square and then,
suddenly, leaps into the "ring". Standing in the corner*

diagonally opposite CEDRIC, JASON *stares, piercingly, at his*
opponent. As the crowd comes back to normal, CREON *steps*
into the center of the "ring".)

CREON: Ladies and Gent, as all you does know,
I win Pecong five time in a row.
Is so!
I, the only livin' Mighty, Royal,
Most Perfect and Grand King Calabash.
Only me daddy 'fore me do what I do...
and win this verbal clash.
But, young Mr. Cedric, here
givin' it a try and he biddin' fair.
So far today, as all you does know,
him done vanquish all him foe.
Him only have this last to go.
Is so!
So, without much further ado
make I present to you,
Mister Jason, the Ram
from the Isle of Tougou.
Yes, him come all the way
from he lickle village...
come all the way here
to t'ief and pillage
the crown quite out from Cedric han'
Yes! Jason of Tougou, the mystery man.
Gentlemen, all you 'proach the center of the combat
zone, if you please.

(CEDRIC and JASON *step to the center of the "ring" to*
receive their instructions and engage in a stare-down.)

CREON: Yes, this Jason come to make invasion
and Cedric a-boil with indignation.
So, on this auspicious occasion,
I goin' judge this conflagration.
I tell you, nobody qualify better than me
to judge and referee.

(The crowd goes wild as CEDRIC *prances around.)*

CREON: Well, all you know the regulation.
You entitle to one legal hesitation.
If you does try for a double...
Oh, man. Trouble, trouble, trouble
on top of trouble.
So, let we have the competition!
No gallavantin'!
Both you shake you hand
and come out chantin'!
Be keen like blade and sharp like pin!
And may the best man win!

PERSIS: That Jason look plenty, plenty sweet in he array.
He look to have plenty heavy stone.
I think I goin' wager a copper or two on he leg, alone.

FAUSTINA: Fool! I tell you what the card say.

PERSIS: Um-hmm, I does hear you...but
somethin' seem to catch me eye
when I see mound that 'tween him thigh!

CREON All you pay 'tention to the gong.
When you hear it sound, begin Pecong!

*(*CREON *hits the gong. Pecong! Music plays. Raucous
Calypso rhythm. The two opponents come out of their
respective corners and dance around each other, feeling each
other out in the manner of boxers, or, if you will, fighting
cocks. The Pecong is a contest in which each man insults
the other. When one man does, the other will react as if he's
been struck by a blow. With each verbal blow, the crowd will
react, as if at a prizefight, and roar its approval.)*

CEDRIC: Came on, Mr. Challenger.
Come, if you dare
Come on, Mr. Big Man.
Come, see how you fare.
Came, come, come.

Take you lickle chance
Make you lickle chant
and then, me word goin' kick you
right in the middle of you shitty pant.

FAUSTINA: Cedric open with wit and style…

JASON: You will pardon me if I does make so bold,
but you empty treat does leave me cold.
I does hear how you is so much "Master",
but me tongue too fast and me brain too faster.
So, Mister Cedric, if you please excuse,
no way-I could lose.

PERSIS: You hear that?

CEDRIC: Well, step up, Boy. If you does dare.
You ain't goin' get a next opportunity so rare.
I just hope you life complete if is me you goin' try to
beat.
Come on, Challenger, but I hope you make you peace
and say you prayer 'fore you heart beat cease…
'cause me word too strong and you blood too thin
to ever 'low you to win!

FAUSTINA: Hahoii? Cedric have it in the bag!

JASON: Treat, treat. treat!
Is all I does hear!
Treat, treat, treat
ringin' in me ear
But when you goin' say? When you goin' do
some damage to this Jason of Tougou?
It look like I goin' have to make the start
and jab you right straight to you heart…
and say, "Cedric, you man of smallish part,
you underarm have odor like ragged fart!"

FAUSTINA: Oh, God!

PERSIS: Whoop!

CEDRIC: I does hear people talk 'bout you
and use bad word, you lout, you
Them does see you seek you pleasure
and all the time, chewin' on the treasure.
I does say, "Stand aside, all you.
Be calm! Don't push
when Jason have he face bury in some young gal
   bush!"

PERSIS: Raucous!

FAUSTINA: Foul utterance!

JASON: It true! I does like them gal so young
and does have them taste on the tip of me tongue.
Bat at night, I does sleep with innocence and joy
because me ain't like you. I ain't sleep with boy!

PERSIS: I, too, enjoyin' this, you know!

CEDRIC: I does see you on the make,
Out there huntin' female snake
with you little tool in you hand
doin' battle
with whatever hole underneath she rattle!

FAUSTINA: A veritable blow!

JASON: And I does see what you does give
to all you sundry relative.
None safe from you...not even you mother,
not even you brother.
You would mate with you sister,
copulate with a Mister.
You would even rape a fever blister!

PERSIS: Cedric reelin'!

FAUSTINA: Shut up!

CEDRIC: You mother behind ain't never see tub.
She mout' nasty and, here the rub,
me too-clean to go 'tween she hip

and I ain't want that ol' haunt lip
nowhere 'round me billy-club.

FAUSTINA: A good return!

JASON: I layin' in me bed. I feel this crunchin'.
quite at me vitals, I feel this munchin!
I pull back me sheet and see you mother lunchin'…
…eh-eh…gnawin' with she rat teeth on me truncheon!

PERSIS: Riposte! Riposte!

CEDRIC: All you family ugly with wart on then face.
Them not even part of the human race!

JASON: You does have the nerve to mention, "face",
when you ugly like a mongoose backin' out a fireplace?

CEDRIC: You mother too crazy for me part
She even see it in she dream.
She does rub it and caress it,
She does reach down and she press it,
but she can't take too much, les' it
make she wet she drawers and scream!

FAUSTINA: Aha! A good hit!

JASON: You mother does quite act like crazy fool.
She jaw go slack and she mout' does drool.
But I think she goin' have to go back to school.
She amateur when it come to nyammin' tool.

CEDRIC: It too bad it have to be this way.
You not so ugly as them all does say.
You know what you face does call to mind?
A wilted, bare-ass, baboon behind
that run into one big meat grind
and lose the fight!
That right!

JASON: I does give you gal friend yardstick.
I fill she to she core,
I tell she, "Me name not Richard!"

but she screamin', "More, Dickie more!"
Then, I does have to fight she
to keep she from me waist.
I box she, then I bite she,
but she screen for lickle more taste!

PERSIS: The boy is a born composer, you hear!

CEDRIC: When last you does have woman?
When last you try it out?
With petite dangle 'tween you leg
that always pointin' sout'.
I does feel so sorry for it,
layin there for dead
while mine jumpin' and mine pumpin'
and you no can raise him head.

JASON: I sorry you let out we secret
I woulda say you can't
But now you done tell the world
you familiar with inside me pant.
I wouldn'ta tell nobody
'cause I ain't want you disgrace
but now all does know
you does bend low
and could tell them how me taste.
I was savin' me nether
for when I get together
with some gal or the other.
But you nyam it all,
bat and ball,
and ain't leave none for you mother

PERSIS: Jason of Tougou pullin' out all the stops!

CEDRIC: I ain't have no time to babble
or hang 'round with no rabble.
I goin' put a end to you once and for all.
I goin' take out me fleshy cutlass

and stick it up you butt, lass,
'cause you cryin' out for bed on which to fall.

FAUSTINA: That ain't such a worthy rhyme, Cedric,

PERSIS: What you card say now?

FAUSTINA: Them say, "Hush you fool mouth!"

JASON: Is me you callin', "Lassie"?
I ain't know you was so classy,
but if you thinkin' I is woman,
you is wrong.
'Cause if you thinkin' you have "slugger"
and is me you try to bugger,
I goin' mash you with somethin' mighty strong
and long.
You surely does mistake me
if you think that you could take me.
You confuse if you think me ass cover with lace,
'Cause I have somethin' here…
You could pet it.
You could pucker you lip,
take you tongue and wet it,
but have a care that me don't let it
rear back he head and spit in you face.

CEDRIC: I…I…I…

PERSIS: Cedric falter! Cedric falter!

CREON: Yes! Cedric does falter!

CEDRIC: Hush you mouth, all you!
All you, shut you yap!
I still have resource
me ain't begin to tap
All you think that Cedric dozin'.
Hah! You got a next think comin'!
I still composin'!
Okay! I got it!
You mother swear she smart

when she latch on to me Part.
She scream and yell,
"Take me to Hell!
I give you everything you think you lack!"
But when me eye glance down
and see what mufflin' 'round,
I send she by sheself
and she ain't come back.

FAUSTINA: Come on, Jason of Tougou. You have him now!

PERSIS: Traitoress!

(JASON *begins a slow, circling stalk.*)

JASON: I layin' in me bed alone.
You mother jump me like dog after bone,
She make a leap. Land 'top me with a crash.
She does mout' me 'till I ain't know which.
I wake up in the mornin' and have private itch.
Is then I see I drippin' and have ugly rash.
And when I go to make wee-wee,
I burn so.. God! I say to she,
'May the bloody pile torment you
and corn grow on you feet
May crab as big as roach
crawl in you bush and eat!
May the whole world turn again' you
and when you a total wreck,
may you fall through you own asshole
and bruck you goddamn neck!

FAUSTINA: Cedric gone now.

PERSIS: Yes. Just like you card does say.

(CEDRIC *staggers. The crowd is silent.* CEDRIC *tries to say words, but they won't came. Of course, nobody can see the veiled figure of* GRANNY ROOT *holding her umbrella over* CEDRIC's *head.* CEDRIC, *unable to speak and disgraced runs*

off in spite of JASON*'s outstretched hand.* GRANNY ROOT
*stays on. There is a great shout from the crowd and the scene
erupts with music and dancing.* CEDRIC*'s band runs after
him.* PERSIS *grabs* JASON *and kisses him.)*

PERSIS: You is one beautiful and elegant lad and you
cause me to win quite a few shekels. You is a born-
Calypsonian! You does have girl friend?

FAUSTINA: I win some, too! He card tell me all along
you was goin' be the winner, so me wager tickle bit of
penny. Move, Woman. Let the man kiss me!

(Before this can happen, however, JASON *is hoisted to the
shoulders of some men and they parade him around.)*

CREON: Young man, I does like you attack
Is through you, me title still intact
You throw Cedric to the ground…and mash he up.
You smartly earn this year Pecong Cup
You is one quite excellent fella
Make I introduce you to me daughter, Sweet Bella

*(*SWEET BELLA *comes forward with a wreath for* JASON*'s
neck. The moment she places it and their eyes meet,*
GRANNY ROOT, *gestures and all except* JASON *and* SWEET
BELLA *seem to freeze.* GRANNY ROOT *sprinkles some dust
into the Pecong Cup and gives it to them, They each drink.*
GRANNY ROOT *retrieves the cup and drains it.* JASON
and SWEET BELLA *begin a slow, sensuous, sinuous dance.
There's not an half-inch of space between them. Even though
the crowd is "frozen", they are not unaware of* SWEET
BELLA *and* JASON*. The impression should be given that
the crowd it moving at a considerably slower pace than the
dancing pair.)*

SWEET BELLA: Jason…

CREON: Me daughter speak!

FAUSTINA, PERSIS, & CROWD: Sweet Bella, the Silent,
speak!

JASON: What sound is this

SWEET BELLA: Jason! Jason!

CREON & ALL: She speak again!

JASON: I ain't never hear a sound so. It like bird! It like bell! It like music! It like Heaven!

SWEET BELLA: Jason!

CREON & ALL: Miracle! Is a miracle!

CREON: The man make me daughter speak! He make she speak! She ain't never 'fore utter sound and she speak when he and she eye meet up. He done bruck the spell cast on she. The man, a prince! Better than a prince. Him a God!

JASON: It feel like I can't speak. It feel like I can't make rhyme. Confusion runnin' wild in me head and elsewhere. Me breath gone! Is like I seein' woman for the first time in me life.

SWEET BELLA: Is not the same with me. I see you before Jason. I see you so many time, I can't count I see you when I wake.
I see you when I sleepin'.
I see you when it sun
or when the moon come creepin'.
I see you in the moon
every moment of me life before.
I swimmin' in the sea.
There ain't no danger to me
because you watchin' me.
You ain't no stranger to me,
I know you comin' soon
Every moment of me life before.
I just find word to say
what I could not express.
Thing people does say every day.
For instance,

word like, "love" and "tenderness"
I see you in me dream
I can't help me dreamin'
I wake up from me dream
and in me heart, I screamin'
Screamin' out you name
and hopin' you just outside me door.
I see you in me eye
In every tear I cry
Each sigh I sigh,
Each lie I lie
In each hello…
In each good-bye
Every moment of me life before
I couldn't speak before
I save me first word for you.
It take me all me life
to tell how I adore you
I ragin' like typhoon
tearin' up the tropic shore,
Yes, I does see you
every moment of me life before
Yes, I see you before, Jason.

JASON: Sweet Bella, I never say this before, I feel to say it now. I does love you. I ain't know why I say it, but I ain't scare to. It just come out. I does love you. It don't even feel strange. I does love you! Yes, that what this feelin' I does feel. Yes! I does love you, Sweet Bella Pandit I does truly love you. I ain't even have more word than that.

(*All the others return to "normal speed".*)

SWEET BELLA: Daddy, I could speak!

CREON: Praise be! I know it was true! Praise be!

(CREON *falls to the ground in gratitude and thanks.*)

SWEET BELLA: Daddy, this man want to talk to you.

CREON: I figure so.

JASON: Mr. Creon Pandit, Mighty, Royal, Most Perfect, Grand King Calabash, all me life I ain't see nobody like you daughter. I know you ain't know nothin' 'bout me, but I not a too bad fellow. In me life, I know a whole lot of gal and I tell you, out in the open, that quite a few does make baby for me. I know me duty to them children, them, and I does do it, but I never feel for none of they mother or any gal, what I does feel for you daughter, Sweet Bella. My heart and entire soul ragin' with flame what like come from the center of the earth. I can't make no procrastination. I say to you before all assemble here. I want to marry you daughter. I want to marry she. Now!

PERSIS: Oh, God! The man fast!

FAUSTINA: The man faster than fast. Him rapid!

JASON: I can't explain what came over me. I see she and me heart just gone.

CREON: It true I ain't know much 'bout you, Jason of Tougou Island. But I does know this. Me daughter born without speech. You does see she for the first time…and she talk. Is a true sign. Is a supernatural occurrence. A true sign from the God, them. Sweet Bella, you want this man?

SWEET BELLA: Is more than just, "want", Daddy. I have to have him. I thinkin'… I feelin'… "If I ain't have he soon, I goin' fall down right at he foot and die and the earth could swallow me and I ain't care a t'ing." I feelin', "If you ain't let me have he and he have me, I goin' climb a scarp or Devil Cliff and pitch meself right into the wind." I feelin', "If I ain't take he soon, I could throw meself right into the flame and When I meet Satan , I would kill he."

PERSIS: Faustina, you ever know such passion was runnin', wild so, inside she?

FAUSTINA: I struck speechless!

CREON: Sweet Bella, you me only child. I ain't never hear you speak before. Even if it a miracle, I can't just throw you to the man. I does just hear you voice, sweet like a bird, for the first time. You want to deprive you daddy of that sweet sound, so soon? Everything makin' fast current, but I ain't a proper daddy if I just...let you go. Of course, this the answer to all me dream. The man have the proper look and coloration and since I ain't have son to carry on me name, I could, at least, have grandson to carry on me blood. And, who know, one day this same grandson could be Mighty, Royal, Most Perfect, Grand King Calabash. Give me three day to make plan and t'ing. Till the end of Carnival. if the two of you still does have no let-upsy, then as magistrate, I, meself, will perform the ceremony just before midnight...last day of Carnival. What you does say, Mister Jason? If you does love she like you does say, three day is a eye-blink.

JASON: Three day is torture! A man could die in three day, but I does love this gal. So, even if it ain't fine with me, she too worth the wait. Okay!

CREON: Well-spoken! Sweet Bella?

(SWEET BELLA *thinks and, finally, nods assent.*)

Don't nod, Gal. You have voice sweeter than mornin' wind in the mountain. Don't deprive you daddy from hearin' it.

SWEET BELLA: Yes, Daddy. I could wait...but three day is all. If you ain't keep you word, I goin' ran off with he, even if it lent! I ain't care.

CREON: Then since all you willin' to wait, I give me consent. I quite happy, you know. Just think, I goin' have me some grandson, at last

(*The crowd erupts! Music! Dancing! Whatever!*)

(*The crowd is at its frenzied peak, when* GRANNY ROOT *comes out of her trance.*)

GRANNY ROOT: Now, we does begin!

(*Thunder! Lightning!* MEDIYAH *appears.*)

MEDIYAH: Jason! Jason! Jason, you son, them, comin'! Come! Hold me hand! Help me! I havin' you son, them, for you, Jason, darlin'.

(*Even* FAUSTINA *and* PERSIS *are speechless.*)

CREON: Jason of Tougou, you does know this woman?

JASON: Yes! I does know she!

CREON: You does know she is sister to Cedric who just fall to you in Pecong?

JASON: No! I ain't ever know that. She ain't ever tell me such!

CREON: You did lay up with she?

JASON: I did lay with she, yes, but no more!

CREON: You ain't love she or promise youself to she?

JASON: Sweet Bella, as the God, them, me judge and witness, I ain't love nobody, but you in the whole of me life, 'side me mother and she long depart from here. This just one of them gal who I does jook up long ago when I was wicked. That, then, Sweetness! I does love you, now, with all the heart you does leave me when you take it so complete.

(MEDIYAH *lets forth a horribly agonizing scream and falls, writhing, on the ground.*)

MEDIYAH: Jason! Jason! Jason, with all you does leave of me heart, I hate you. I does curse you and before all here, I swear I goin' have me vengeance. Aaaiiieee!!!

GRANNY ROOT: Aha! You Granny Root granddaughter again.

MEDIYAH: Aaaiiieee!!! Granny! Granny, call all the God, them. Attend me!

CREON: She delirious! She talkin' to she dead Granny! she talkin' to air!

PERSIS: All you hard-back man, get 'way from here. Go stand some place and hide you eye. All you woman, surround me. And one of you, tear off you petticoat and give me.

(The men obey, as do the women, encircling MEDIYAH, *being attended by* FAUSTINA *and* PERSIS. JASON *and* SWEET BELLA *stand off, alone.* CREON *stands apart, watching them.)*

SWEET BELLA: I does love you, Jason of Tougou. I ain't give a care what you do before I see you. I sorry for Mediyah, but you does belong to me. I sorry for she, but I ain't care. I does love you.

JASON: I does love you, Sweet Bella Pandit.

SWEET BELLA: Three day, Jason! Three day 'till Carnival end and then, I goin' have you.

JASON: Three day!

SWEET BELLA: Just 'fore midnight on Carnival Night! 'Fore four-Day Mornin' come in sight!

JASON: Oh, God!

*(*SWEET BELLA *walks off, leaving* JASON. GRANNY ROOT *passes her umbrella over the crowd. There is an audible gasp. Seconds later, there is another.* PERSIS, *after a bit, approaches* JASON *carrying two petticoat-wrapped bundles.* JASON *is allowed to see the contents of the bundles, but when*

he reaches for them, PERSIS *pulls back.* JASON *walks off.*
GRANNY ROOT *passes her umbrella over* CREON's *head. He
starts, frightened.)*

(Looking over his shoulder, CREON *goes.)*

GRANNY ROOT: Yes, Mediyah. You hatred make you
Granny Root granddaughter, again.

*(*GRANNY ROOT *cackles. Lights go out.)*

Scene Three

*(*MEDIYAH's *hut and it's still far from neat.* MEDIYAH,
on her mallet, stares into space. GRANNY ROOT, *eyes
focused on her granddaughter, stirs some- thing in a
pot. Two rough-hewn cradles are in evidence.)*

GRANNY ROOT: You brother comin'.

MEDIYAH: I know.

*(*CEDRIC, *drunk and angry, enters. He surveys the condition
of the hut and his sister. His eyes alight on the two cradles.)*

CEDRIC: So, it true! You make two baby! I does hear
'bout it from all who get ecstasy when they could
spread ondit! And you name in everybody mouth. I
now see why you say you can't help me to get wood
for a next quatro. You pitch over you own brother for
help some man who ain't give a fart for you. He load
you up with pickney, them, and then he cut out. Right
now, he languishin' in the arm of Sweet Bella Pandit.
Right now, he croonin' lilt in she ear…the same like he
mussie done to you. Right now, he t'unpin all we half-
sister. Right now, you ain't even in he memory, 'cause
he too busy addin' another notch to he count. Good for
you!

*(*GRANNY ROOT *gestures to silent* CEDRIC, *but* MEDIYAH,
*her eyes still rooted in space, raises her hand to indicate that
she wants* CEDRIC *to talk on.)*

CEDRIC: You know what that man do to me? This man who you lay on you back for. You know what him do? Him shame me! Him cause me to cast me head down and not be able for lift it. Him cause everybody, who did have respect and fear for me, to laugh and stamp them foot with glee as I does pass. He does cause everybody to have only toleration for me like they does have for bug! You know how that does feel? Well, I hope you know it soon. I curse you, Sister! I hope you blood and you milk does turn to ugly, hellacious green bile. I hope you body dry up and turn to black powder. You help to kill you brother, obdiyah. It like I tear up into lickle piece and throw to dog for eat. I hope both you boy know the pain you cause me. I could have be like king in this place, but you abdicate me. Damn you, Sister! Damn you! *(He, drunkenly, stumbles out.)*

GRANNY ROOT: Too bad!

MEDIYAH: Part of Cedric curse already true. Ain't nothin' runnin' through me vein but bile and bitterness.

GRANNY ROOT: You need more than bitterness.

MEDIYAH: I know.

GRANNY ROOT: I know you know, but I makin' sure. *(She tastes her concoction.)*

It ready. I even put in some t'ing even you ain't know 'bout. You had long sleep. I had was to wait for you to wake. I ain't even able to talk to you in you dream.

MEDIYAH: I ain't need you in me dream. Only room in me dream for me hatred of Jason of Tougou.

GRANNY ROOT: Jason is man...and man does inspire hatred. Tell me hatred done replace love in you heart. Tell me hatred of man does replace love in you heart!

MEDIYAH: I done told you!

GRANNY ROOT: No! You tell me hatred of Jason. Tell me, now, is hatred of man you feelin'

MEDIYAH: Yes!

GRANNY ROOT: Tell me again and swear it!

(GRANNY ROOT *grabs* MEDIYAH's *hands and spits in the palm of each.*)

Swear it!

MEDIYAH: I does swear it! By all the God, them, I does swear it!

GRANNY ROOT: Good! Aha! Right on time.

(FAUSTINA *and* PERSIS *enter.*)

PERSIS: Mediyah! Mediyah!

FAUSTINA: Mediyah, we could come in?

MEDIYAH: Yes.

PERSIS: Thank you. How the two little baby keepin'?

MEDIYAH: Them sleep!

PERSIS: And we shoutin' and keepin' noise and t'ing.

FAUSTINA: Shame on you!

MEDIYAH: Is all right. They does sleep sound. They ain't wake 'till them want to.

PERSIS: Is always such a joy to have tickle baby cryin' in the house.

MEDIYAH: Them don't cry! Baby only cry 'cause them can't tell you what do they' I know what do these two, so them don't have for cry. They ain't cry when them born and them never goin' cry.

PERSIS: As long as them have them health…that what count, I suppose,

FAUSTINA: Mediyah, we could help you pick up 'round here?

PERSIS: We could do so, if you want for we to do so. I mean, we ain't want for interfere, but if you does need some help to…

MEDIYAH: Why all you does want to do this. All we ain't friend! I does thank you for deliverin' the baby, them, but we ain't waste no love or like on weself.

FAUSTINA: Mediyah, is time we does put all this ruction aside, The man do you a horrendous dirtiness. I never see such in all me life.

PERSIS: Never! You deliverin' the man baby. Two of them…as if one ain't hard enough. You twitchin' in the dirt and he rejectin' you right on the self-same spot.

FAUSTINA: It like he grab hold of all we woman and slap all we. It like he rainin' blow on all we arse!

MEDIYAH: You come to tell me this?

FAUSTINA: We come to tell you that Creon Pandit makin' big weddin' plan for he daughter and that rapscallion who did have he way with you,

PERSIS: Them goin' marry at Carnival finish tomorrow night!

FAUSTINA: Before midnight! It goin' be the highlight

PERSIS: But even worse…

FAUSTINA: …The man on he way here now…

PERSIS: …Comin' to you hut for…

MEDIYAH: He comin' for take he two son 'way from here.

PERSIS: You does know this?

FAUSTINA: You ain't goin' 'low he to have he way?

PERSIS: No! You couldn't condone such action.

FAUSTINA: No! I ain't goin' believe that!

MEDIYAH: I say what I goin' do?

FAUSTINA: But you does have a certain look in you eye that does say…

MEDIYAH: You does see look in me eye? I ain't know you could see look in me eye. But you is most observant. Keep lookin' in me eye! That right! Both you keep lookin' in me eye. Closer, Ladies.

(FAUSTINA and PERSIS are "enchanted".)

GRANNY ROOT: Yes, Granddaughter, you does have you power back.

MEDIYAH: Now, all you go wait just outside 'till I does call you to come in.

FAUSTINA & PERSIS: Yes, Mediyah

(Obediently, FAUSTINA and PERSIS go.)

MEDIYAH: You does know me mind?

GRANNY ROOT: Yes! Steel youself. He comin'.

MEDIYAH: I know!

(JASON enters, wearing the suit MEDIYAH bought him.)

JASON: Hello!

MEDIYAH: Jason.

JASON: You does feel all right?

MEDIYAH: I fine! I ain't perform no feat! I ain't do nothin' ain't ordinary. I only have twin…for you. Nothin' special.

JASON: I see them two woman outside you place dawdlin' 'round.

MEDIYAH: Them help deliver you son, them. Them came to inquire after they health. That what you a-come for?

JASON: Mediyah, you still have this place unkempt. Well, I ain't come to lash you with more word over you bad housekeepin'. I goin' be brief. You does know I fall in love with Sweet Bella Pandit and does plan to marry up with she 'fore Lent Mornin' come.

MEDIYAH: Is so I did hear. I offer me congrats.

JASON: You ain't vex?

MEDIYAH: Why I should vex? You ain't love me. I distapoint true...but I ain't vex.. no more. I find you on Miedo Wood Island all hack up and wrack up. True! I heal you and comfort you. True! I give you wood and wildcat gut for fashion quatro for you to win Pecong. True! I give you two boy you say you want for so long and never have. All that true, but I ain't vex. Why should I vex?

JASON: Good! I glad you does feel so, 'cause I ain't want to make you no hurt. Well, as you does say, I always want some son. Now, I does have them and, now, I does want them.

MEDIYAH: With you!

JASON: With me! Boy belong with them daddy!

MEDIYAH: Them ain't nowhere yet near wean.

JASON: If you had kick out, them two boy would have to find some other woman to give them titty. I win Pecong. I have lickle cash to buy fertile titty from woman in that business. You ain't truly want them boy, you know. You ain't need no reminder of me. I just a scalawag, you know, and it best you does forget me.

MEDIYAH: You will pardon me, Jason, but I ain't never goin' forget you.

JASON: Well, I ain't see how you could, but me charm aside, the boy, them, goin' be better off with me. I marryin' well and Creon does like me.

MEDIYAH: Of course! You make he daughter chatter after a life of silence and you does have good tint.

Match it with he Sweet Bella and the two of you could make grandchild with pleasin' coloration.

JASON: True!

MEDIYAH: What about these two boy.

JASON: Them fair enough, thanks to me. Them ain't goin' get too much darker 'cause I did peek at them ear when them birth.

MEDIYAH: I see.

JASON: Anyway, them goin' be taken good care of. So, give me them, nuh!

MEDIYAH: Them goin' soon wake up and want the milk. You better leave me nurse them a next time. You could go someplace and then, come back after them suck. Then you could have them.

JASON: You ain't goin' give me trouble?

MEDIYAH: Why I should do such? What you does say, true! Boy belong with them Daddy. I ain't carve out to be mother. 'Specially to you children. Look how I does keep this place. Like you say, you ain't want no son from you…raise in pig sty.

JASON: True!

MEDIYAH: True! So, you go, take a trot, then, come back and…

JASON: I know you was goin' have good sense. Sweet Bella tell me you was goin' cause some aggravation 'bout this. I tell she, she wrong 'cause I does know you.

MEDIYAH: But, she ain't know me. I ain't goin' cause no excitement. I, too, glad she talkin', you know.

JASON: You ain't upset with she?

MEDIYAH: You look at she, she look at you and she speak. That a great amen. A sign from up there. I can't find no fault with what the God, them, does decree.

What happen ain't she fault. And I no more upset with
she than I upset with you. All you want is for raise up
you son, them. True?

JASON: True! Give them they last milk and I goin' come
back. Oh, yes. I did never thank you for the quatro. So,
I do it now. Thank you!

MEDIYAH: Oh, you most welcome. Thank you for the
twin!

JASON: You welcome, too. *(He goes.)*

GRANNY ROOT: Worthless dog! Vile pig!

MEDIYAH: Granny, what dog and pig do to you, you
does insult they so?

GRANNY ROOT: I make apology to all the animal I
confuse he with. It all I could do to keep from doin'
somethin' to he.

MEDIYAH: Mister Jason of Tougou
I goin' get marry, too.
I sendin' you a special invite
to me nuptial night!
Since you special, I makin' room
for you, right 'tween me and me groom.

GRANNY ROOT: Hahoiii!!! Give youself over, Girl!

MEDIYAH: Come to me, All you God from the old
country and the old time.
Come to me and make me harder. Steel me!
God of Thunder, speak in your most angry temper!
God of Lightning, wreak you havoc and illuminate the
darkest hour with you blindin' power!
God of Wind, be extreme in you violence and blow the
path of gentility to Hell,
God of Cold, plant icy river in me heart.
God of Hell, attend me!
Sun, Moon, Star, hide you face and let through
the God of Vengeance

to marry and consummate with me
and spew Use foul content of we marriage bed
over Sweet Bella Pandit
and that bastard thing she choose for sheself.
Make me blood like hot oil
to burn and smother all life
from they and all they line!
Fill me with hate
and let that hate never depart!
God of Vengeance, stay with me forever!
God of Hate, stay with me forever!
God of Screamin' Quiet and Quiet Scream,
Be all my life
God of Vengeance and Hate, make me you wife!
(She goes to the cradle and regards the inhabitants.)
And for these…
…these that come from them two regrettable seed he
plant in me,
make me milk
pure boilin', bubblin', bitter and burnin' bane.
*(She picks up the babies and places them, one at each breast.
Lights swirl, flicker and dim.)*
Now, Jason, you can come for you two boy.
Take they to you bride and enjoy.

GRANNY ROOT: You do well, me daughter. You please
all the old God, them and you please Granny, too!

(GRANNY ROOT laughs, malevolently, lights.)

Scene Four

*(MEDIYAH's hut. Moments later. She has nursed the babies
and returned then to their cradles. She goes to the doorway.)*

MEDIYAH: Attend me here!

*(PERSIS and FAUSTINA, obediently, enter and, drinking
from wooden goblets offered them by MEDIYAH, sit as she*

directs. GRANNY ROOT *indicates by gesture that* JASON
approaches.)

MEDIYAH: I know! Come in, Jason. These two lady help
deliver you baby. They not only have plenty interest,
but them does have plenty milk. They does, therefore,
provide one pair of titty for each one you boy. If you
ain't want them, you ain't get the baby, them. Agree?

JASON: Agree!

MEDIYAH: Good!

JASON: You two ain't mind?

PERSIS: No! How we could mind?

FAUSTINA: No way we could mind.

FAUSTINA & PERSIS: In fact, we quite "enchant" to do
such!

JASON: Good! I sure make two healthy lookin' boy. I
think they goin' suck you dry within the week.

MEDIYAH: Jason, if you ain't mind, I have weddin' gift
for you bride. Is to show you and she me heart in the
right place. I guess you want know what inside. I tell
you. Is a think I purchase in Creon store, A night frock
so pretty and silky, I did plan to wear it on me weddin'
night…if you did ever so choose to marry up with me.
But, you ain't choose to marry up with me so, I think
Sweet Bella should have it. At least, it still serve a
bride. I put thousand petal from flower and quite some
sweet herb in the parcel to give it scent and wishes for
the future.

JASON: Flower and herb?

MEDIYAH: Yes. I had mean to enchant you like any
young gal on she night of night would enchant she
princely groom, but since that rule out, Sweet Bella will
wear it and, maybe, take you to Paradise.

JASON: On she behalf, I does thank you. Is a kind and gentle gesture. You does surprise me.

MEDIYAH: Jason, I goin' turn me back. Persis! Faustina! Take the baby and go with he. When I turn 'round, I ain't want to see none of you here. Go!

JASON: You two lady, *suivez-moi!* Good-bye, Mediyah! I ain't expect to see you a next time. I think you goin' have it much better if you ain't stay in this place. If you ain't think of youself, think of these two boy. Yes! It goin' go much better for you, if you leave here. Remember, the magistrate goin' be me father-in-law! Good-bye!

(FAUSTINA *and* PERSIS *gather the two babes and follow* JASON, *who carries the "gift".*)

GRANNY ROOT: Death! I wishin' a hard and evil and fast death to Jason of Tougou.

MEDIYAH: No! I ain't goin permit that! Take back you wish! It wasted on he. I alread see to it that Jason of Tougou goin' live. He goin' have the most long and most slow life of remembrance. Now, Granny, content youself in some business or whatever you please. I goin' sit here and 'wait the news.

(*As* GRANNY ROOT *eyes her,* MEDIYAH *arranges herself to receive the news. She stares, vacantly, humming to herself as she rocks...and waits.*)

Scene Five

(*Darkness. There are screams of utmost horror. Townspeople run to and fro in utter confusion. The lights come up to reveal,* MEDIYAH, *sitting impassively and,* GRANNY ROOT, *anxious to swallow every word from* PERSIS *and* FAUSTINA, *who come running up, exhausted, in tears and filled with revulsion.*)

PERSIS: Oh, Mediyah...

FAUSTINA: Oh, God! Mediyah! Mediyah!

PERSIS: How could you manipulate we so?
How you could do such?

FAUSTINA: How? How? How? How you could hate so
much?

PERSIS: Oh, Mediyah, you is one hard,

FAUSTINA: Harsh,

PERSIS: Bitter,

FAUSTINA: Sour woman!

(MEDIYAH *sits like a stone.*)

MEDIYAH: You will relate the event

PERSIS: Me and Faustina find weself in Creon Pandit
house. We does hear some laughter and we realize, the
weddin' festivity afoot.

FAUSTINA: For we part, we ain't know how we get
there. It like me and Persis wakin' from some dream.
We in some room. Everything sorta haze and we eye
gettin' 'custom to we surroundin', when we doe each
feel somethin' strange.

PERSIS: Both of we scream out simultaneous.
Both of we look down.
Both of we does have one pitiful baby at we breast.
Baby all purple and discolor.
Two baby who ain't ask for this world.
Two baby,
Dead!

FAUSTINA: We scream and scream and scream and
scream and scream.

(*In the background, under separate spotlights,* JASON *and*
CREON *appear...to mime out the action.*)

FAUSTINA:
And Creon and Jason of Tougou come runnin'
and bruck down the door and,
still in them weddin' costume,
cutlass in hand,
whoosh in!
Them see the baby in we arm.

PERSIS: The dead baby in we arm.

FAUSTINA: Jason fall down with horrible cry-out
and thrash the floor.
He knuckle bleed as he whimper to Heaven,
"Why?", "Why?", "Why?"

PERSIS: I never hear man cry with such agony and
sorriness.

FAUSTINA:
Creon grab we and shake we and yell, so, at we
that we does kill these two baby.
When we does tell he we ain't know what happen,
or how these baby does come to be dead,
Jason jump up and attack we.
He cutlass swingin' and flingin'
and flailin' and sailin' in the air.

PERSIS: The only reason he metal ain't seriously catch
we, is all the tear in he eye leave he foot unsteady and
him aim faulty.

PERSIS: Then, we hear a sound. A scream,
so high,
so sharp,
so pierce,
More keen than blade.
It halt Jason in he track
and cause all we to stand stiller than death!
When all we leg free, we run to that scream
that even God would fear.
It comin' from the nuptial chamber.

We pitch open the portal
and, oh, what we see!

FAUSTINA & PERSIS: Oh, God! What we see!
What we see!
What we see!

(SWEET BELLA, *her nightdress aflame, writhes and screams in excruciating agony.*)

FAUSTINA: Sweet Bella have on the very night frock you gift she with.
Sweet Bella. It seem only a few hour since she find she voice

PERSIS: Sweet Bella. She voice so sweet
and so like a little bell that tinkle.
Sweet Bella. She voice, now like a grate.
Yellin' and roarin' and grindin' and raspin'

FAUSTINA & PERSIS: And she body…aflame!
Aflame! Aflame!
She entire body aflame!

FAUSTINA: Creon pitch heself on he daughter.

PERSIS: Jason…pitch heself on he bride
and he new in-law daddy.
But the flame too hot and mighty.
Creon burn too bad,
but him stay clamp to he daughter
in they incestuous dance to the death.
Jason…fall away
screamin' with no sound from he mouth.
It too late.

FAUSTINA: What use to be Sweet Bella
now only ash and dust and smoke and steam
and burn flesh and smell that does make you
sick to you bowel.

PERSIS: A stench like you never smell.

FAUSTINA: Creon, burn and disfigure,
skin meltin' 'way from he carcass,
run and stagger 'till he leg no longer carry he.
He fall 'pon top Sweet Bella and
mash she corpse to charcoal.
He last breath come from he mouth like a sad whistle...
and he pass into history.

PERSIS: Oh, Mediyah, what that gal do to you?
What she do to you, so bad she earn such a dispatch?
What Creon do, so bad, he no longer have breath
to breathe?

FAUSTINA & PERSIS: Ah, Mediyah, you a hard, harsh,
bitter, sour woman!

MEDIYAH: *(Stonily)* What of Jason?

PERSIS: We comin' to that.

FAUSTINA: But we have a next bitter news.

FAUSTINA & PERSIS: Tragedy 'pon tragedy.
Sorrow 'pon sorrow.
Bitterness 'pon bitterness.
Sadness 'pon sadness

PERSIS: And strangeness...'pon strangeness for as we
runnin' here to tell you all this occurrence, we see,
Cedric, you brother.

(In the background, CEDRIC *appears dangling.)*

FAUSTINA: Cedric, the Rhymer, now defeated.
In he hand, he quatro mangle
He eye...agape and starin' straight to Heaven
and he once proud body, dangle
...dangle from a tree
where there were no tree before.

PERSIS A calabash tree that spring up overnight.

*(*CEDRIC *disappears.)*

MEDIYAH: What of Jason?

PERSIS: Woman, you can't take lickle time to mourn the dead?

FAUSTINA: You have no sorrow for none of these people?

FAUSTINA & PERSIS: Poor Mediyah. You is a hard, harsh, bitter, sour woman!

MEDIYAH: What of Jason?

FAUSTINA & PERSIS:
We only have sorrow and sadness for you.
Such a hard, harsh, bitter, sour woman!
Pity! Pity! Pity!

MEDIYAH: What about Jason of Tougou?

PERSIS: Jason? That poor waste man?
Jason, as we say, thrash heself on the ground.
Be eye shed more water than Yama Waterfall.

FAUSTINA: More than the river.

PERSIS:
Then it dawn on he that he should dead like Creon,
'cause he ain't nothin' more to live for,
but he ain't have the courage to bear the pain
and grab it like Creon.
And he commence to reprimand heself
with blow after blow
and he run 'bout the room
pitchin' heself 'gainst all four wall.
I never see such a pitiful madness.

FAUSTINA: Then, with brutal suddenness, him halt!
Him livid and turn this dull blue and gray tint
right in front of we very eye.
He body and he glance grow cold.
A cold like we never feel in this island.
We had was to grab shawl and throw 'bout we shoulder,
the man radiate such cold.

Then, he walk over to them what use to have life
and he look down.
Be come over to we,
for we still have he dead, shrivel-up, baby, them
in we arm.
He relieve we of them
and he look down.
Then, he give they back to we
and he look down.

PERSIS: Then, he pick up he shiny machette
and say to we,

JASON: Go! Tell the witch, Mediyah, to prepare sheself!
Tell she I comin' with heavy, ponderous, sorrowful,
    sad
and deliberate footstep to kill she!
To rid this Door world of she!
To send she back to the very bowel of Hell
from which she spring!
Go! Tell she all this!
Tell she, who grind and mash and tear and break
and poison and burn me heart,
all this! Go!

PERSIS: Is so him say and is so we do!
All we beg you leave to go.
Please don't trouble youself to show
further botheration for we.

FAUSTINA:
If, perchance, you does see we takin' we custom,
please to turn you head
and treat we like people dead
and gone.

FAUSTINA & PERSIS:
You cause we eye to be full with tear
and we heart be heavy with stone

and youself to be forever…alone!
Good-bye!

(FAUSTINA and PERSIS, *tearfully, leave.* MEDIYAH *and*
GRANNY ROOT *sit in respective attitudes of impassiveness
and waiting. In the distance, a drum beat, signaling
approaching heavy footsteps. Soft, muted and measured at
first, their sound gets louder and louder until, at last,* JASON
fills the door frame with himself. MEDIYAH, *defiant, turns
to face him. He raises his weapon, grasping the hilt with
both hands, high over his head as if to cleave the stone-faced*
MEDIYAH *in two.*)

JASON (*Screaming.*) MEDIYAH!!!!!!!!

(JASON *brings down his machete with all his might and
purpose, but the blade stops inches above the head of*
MEDIYAH, *whose gaze continues to "fix" him. Whimpering,
he slowly crumples to the floor in an abject heap. On
his knees and at the feet of* MEDIYAH, *she, slowly and
disdainfully, raises a foot and, scornfully, pushes him over…
leaving him prostrate and sobbing.*)

JASON: Mediyah! Mediyah! Mediyah!

(MEDIYAH *begins a slow, circular walk with* JASON
crawling, abjectly and snake-like, after her.)

MEDIYAH: And is so you will be from now. A crawlin',
grovelin', slitherin' thing that people does see and set
them dog on and spit at. 'Low me, if you please, to be
the first.
(*She spits at him.*)
You did cause me some pain and hurt.
So, forever eat sand and mud and dirt!
Eat dust and t'ing what does drop from dog!
Eat worm and t'ing what does hide 'neath log!
Yes! Know only sand and mud and dirt!
Raise you head only high as the hem of me skirt!
Stay down in the gravel where you does belong,
Jason of Tougou, master of Pecong!

Master of lilt! Master of rhyme!
Master of filt'! Master of crime!
As long as you does continue to be,
You ain't never, never, never, ever goin' forget me!
Wherever you crawlin' take you,
be it far or be it near,
Make you take you this name for carry
forever in you ear...
(*She bends down and screams in his ear...*)
"MEDIYAH!!!"

(MEDIYAH, *disdainfully, points him toward the door.*
Painfully, slowly and still sobbing, JASON, *crawls on his*
belly, from the scene.)

GRANNY ROOT: It all done now. You revenge. All man
what does do you harshness...gone! My daughter, you
Mother, revenge! Creon and all he line...gone! There
ain't goin' never be a next Creon Pandit!

MEDIYAH: All Creon line not gone. I still here.

GRANNY ROOT:
You ain't Creon seed. You different seed from Cedric.
You all herb and bush and root and air and fire and
    smoke
and earth and wild forest.
You want to see you Daddy?
You want to see who spew heself forth into you mother
at my prayin' and incantation
so she shame could be avenge?
You want to see who cause you to birth?
Behold! Behold!

(GRANNY ROOT *gestures. Smoke! Thunder! Lightning!*
Fire! The awesome figure of Damballah appears and
menacingly, but silently, laughs. Be dances...prances...a
puff of smoke and he disappears.)

GRANNY ROOT: When you mother come to me
and say she power gone,

She beg me not to damn he,
for she so love he, this Creon.
But Granny Root pray
and Granny Root "do".
Spirit appear...
and, out come...you!
You...all Granny Root perception.
You...all spiritual conception.
You...all Granny Root revenge.
You...all Granny Root say you was
and...that all you was.
Come!
You and me off to Miedo Wood Island.
Is we home.

MEDIYAH: So! That Jason I did love
and that Jason I did hate.
Now, I ain't feel nothin' for he
'cause me passion bate.
I ain't feel he a-tall!
I ain't feel nothin' a-tall!

GRANNY ROOT: To Miedo Wood Island, Child.
You and me goin' say we "Good-bye" There.
Me spirit tire and me can sleep...now!

(GRANNY ROOT and MEDIYAH disappear.)

Epilogue

(A group of revelers, stragglers from Carnival, noisily
crosses the scene. Still dancing and swilling from rumpots,
they're drunkenly trying to keep the spirit going. PERSIS and
FAUSTINA open their slatted windows.)

PERSIS: All you...less that noise! You ain't know what
time it is?

FAUSTINA: You ain't know what day it is? Carnival
over! It Lent and Carnival over!

PERSIS: You ain't know that?

FAUSTINA: What do you?

FAUSTINA & PERSIS: Is time for all you 'semble here
to low you eye and be austere.
Go home! Go home! Until next year
Carnival over! You hear?

(The revelers reflect for a moment, wave off PERSIS *and* FAUSTINA *and go off, still shuffling to their beat. Still drinking in the morning heat.* PERSIS *and* FAUSTINA, *regard them, shrug their shoulders, regard each other, shrug their shoulders and go off to join the merry band.)*

END OF PLAY

CPSIA information can be obtained
at www.ICGtesting.com
Printed in the USA
LVHW051941301219
642078LV00016B/1858

9 780881 451078